Everything
You Need
to Know

Iran

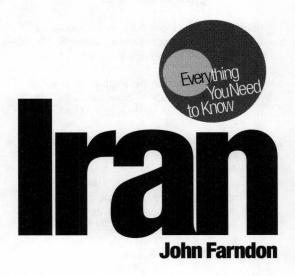

Everything
You Need
to Know

Iran

John Farndon

ICON BOOKS

Published in the UK in 2006 by Icon Books Ltd,
The Old Dairy, Brook Road, Thriplow,
Cambridge SG8 7RG
email: info@iconbooks.co.uk
www.iconbooks.co.uk

Sold in the UK, Europe, South Africa and Asia
by Faber & Faber Ltd, 3 Queen Square, London WC1N 3AU
or their agents

Distributed in the UK, Europe, South Africa and Asia
by TBS Ltd, TBS Distribution Centre, Colchester Road
Frating Green, Colchester CO7 7DW

Published in Australia in 2006
by Allen & Unwin Pty Ltd, PO Box 8500,
83 Alexander Street, Crows Nest, NSW 2065

Distributed in Canada by Penguin Books Canada,
90 Eglinton Avenue East, Suite 700,
Toronto, Ontario M4P 2YE

ISBN 10: 1-84046-776-2
ISBN 13: 978-1840467-76-5

Text copyright © 2006 John Farndon

Typesetting by Wayzgoose
Printed and bound in the UK by Bookmarque

Contents

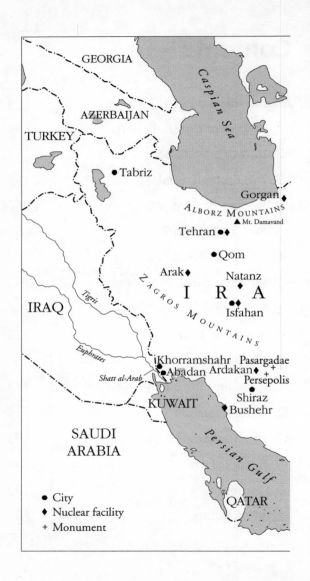

GEORGIA

Caspian Sea

AZERBAIJAN

TURKEY

●Tabriz

Gorgan◆

ALBORZ MOUNTAINS
▲Mt. Damavand

Tehran●◆

●Qom

Arak◆   Natanz
                  ◆
I   R   ◆   A

Isfahan◆●

IRAQ

Tigris

Euphrates

Khorramshahr Pasargadae
●Abadan Ardakan◆   +
Shatt al-Arab   Persepolis
                      ●
KUWAIT   Shiraz
         ◆Bushehr

SAUDI
ARABIA

Persian Gulf

● City
◆ Nuclear facility
+ Monument

QATAR

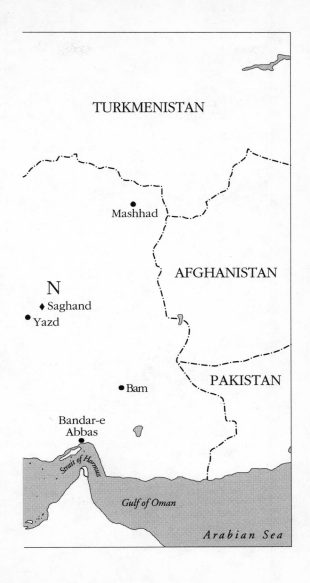

CHAPTER 1

A Mass of Contradictions

'As the Imam said, Israel must be wiped off the map.'
President Ahmadinejad of Iran, October 2005

When Iran's newly-elected President Ahmadinejad made this disturbing outburst about the destruction of Israel, it came as no surprise, of course, to Iran's critics. It was abundantly clear to them that after a brief flirtation with reform under previous president Muhammad Khatami, Iran had swung back into the hands of the Islamic hardliners with Ahmadinejad's victory in August 2005 – and the new president's remarks seemed only to confirm their worst fears. For its critics, Iran has become a pariah state – a loose cannon under the control of fanatical mullahs that could bring havoc and discord to the Middle East.

The hawks in the US government in particular have made no secret of their distrust of Iran. During his first term as President, George W. Bush famously cited Iran as part of his 'Axis of Evil' along with Iraq and North Korea. And in the inaugural speech for his second term, Bush made a point of denouncing Iran as the 'world's primary sponsor of state terror'. At other times, Vice President Dick Cheney has assured us that 'Iran is at the top of the list' when it comes to the world's danger spots.

The nuclear crisis

No wonder, then, that when, in early 2006, Iran announced that it would press ahead with its plans to develop nuclear power in the teeth of inter-national opposition, many feared the worst. Iran has the world's second-largest oil reserves. So what could they possibly want with nuclear power?, crit-ics ask. The answer to them is blindingly obvious: it's not nuclear power that Iran really wants, but nuclear weapons. And an Iran armed with nuclear weapons threatening to wipe Israel off the map would be a frightening prospect indeed.

As attempts to put pressure on Iran to comply with its obligations under the Nuclear Non-proliferation Treaty (NPT) began to run into trouble in spring 2006, politicians in the US and UK governments were challenged by the press to deny that they were considering military action against Iran. In an interview with BBC Radio Four's *Today* programme (13 March 2006), British Foreign Secretary Jack Straw insisted that military action against Iran was 'inconceivable', but acknowledged that with the USA 'nothing is ever ruled out'. Straw also insisted that an Iran armed with nuclear weapons would be 'a serious danger to the balance of power in the Middle East'.

All the other major signatories of the NPT – including, significantly, Russia and China – are critical of Iran's stance on nuclear power. Yet many people feel that the view of Iran taken by the hardliners in the Bush government is seriously blinkered. Moreover, they worry that this blinkered view is raising the stakes and reducing the chances of a successful diplomatic outcome. As Stephen Kinzer of the *New York Times* says: 'The militancy of many of [Iran's] leaders, and that of many of their counterparts in Washington, has sharply reduced the chances of compromise. Without such compromise, however, Iran may find itself in the centre of a global crisis.'

> An unnamed senior Iranian official, quoted in the *New York Times*, 15 March 2006: 'For 27 years after the [Islamic] revolution, America wanted to get Iran to the [UN] Security Council and America failed. Ahmadinejad did that.'

There's no doubt that many Iranians are deeply unhappy about the Bush government's view of their country. They are amazed, and not a little insulted, by the assumption that they are Arabs like their neighbours Iraq. They are a unique people, speaking their own language (Farsi), with their own remarkable culture. And unlike some of their neighbouring states, Iran is not an arbitrary nation created by European colonialists drawing lines on maps. It's an ancient nation, with a rich history dating back 2,500 years.

Persia or Iran?

Of course, for most its history, Iran was known in the West by its Greek name of Persia. It has been known abroad as Iran only since the 1920s – although Iran is what most of its own people always called it. And Persia and Iran both conjure up rather different stock images. Talk of Persia, and many people in the West get an instant picture of a dreamy, ancient, glamorous empire – a land of beautiful magic carpets, secret, fountain-filled gardens, roses and shiraz grapes, luxurious fabrics and harems where dark-eyed beauties lounge around. The Persians in this image may be given to sensual pleasures, but are of course, the cliché goes, immensely civilised and polite. Talk of Iran, however, and many people instantly think of a dour, rabidly puritanical country led by fanatical, black-clad mullahs, all too ready to urge destruction on non-believers. Yet Persia and Iran are the same country, and while both these contradictory images are travesties, there is a grain of truth in both. This is what makes Iran difficult for outsiders to read.

Iran is a deeply contradictory country. It is at once one of the oldest countries in the world and the youngest. Its roots date back through a 2,500-year line of kings to Cyrus the Great, who unified the country in the 6th century BC, and many Iranians today proudly acknowledge their descent from the first Persians. All over Iran are wonderful ancient buildings, from the great ruined city of Persepolis to the wind-towers of

Yazd. The great square and mosques of Isfahan are among the greatest historical sites in the world.

The last king, Muhammad Reza Shah, was overthrown in 1979 by the remarkable Islamic Revolution, which gave control of the country to the Islamic clerics headed by Ayatollah Khomeini. The change in the country was, at least on the surface, so dramatic that it was almost as if the country was born anew. To an extent, this is almost literally true. There was such a population explosion in the decade following the 1979 revolution that Iran's population virtually doubled, and almost half of Iranians are now under 25 – so young that the Iran of the Islamic Revolution is all they have ever known. Much of the physical fabric of the country is almost equally new. In Tehran in particular, many of the old buildings have been demolished to make way for a gigantic sprawl of concrete apartment blocks that make the city, just a village little more than a century ago, bigger than New York.

At the heart of Iranian life is what at first seems to be another massive contradiction. There is a genuine pride in the glory days of the Persian empire before the coming of Islam in the 6th century, and many widely celebrated seasonal festivals date from this time, such as the Iranian

New Year or No Ruz. Yet the coming of Islam profoundly changed the country, and most Iranians remain devout Muslims. When the last shah was in power, he cultivated the country's pre-Islamic Persian heritage at the expense of Islam. Now the Islamic clerics are in power, they frown upon the Persian days – and have tried to destroy some of the most famous Persian monuments. So, some people ask, which is the true Iran – sensual Persia or fervidly puritanical Islam? The answer may be, for most Iranians, a bit of both.

Sceptical believers

Today, Iran is gripped by the tyrannical rule of the Islamic hardliners. Dissent is crushed. Troublesome people disappear. Provocative books are banned. Most women are hidden behind the thick veil of the chador when they go out. America is regarded as the Great Satan, and Israel an abomination. The Iranian regime supports organisations with terrorist links such as Hezbollah, and is accused by some of fomenting the unrest in Iraq. Yet more women go to university than in most Western countries. The reformist young Iranians listen to Western music, follow Western fashions and exchange ideas over the internet with an energy and enthusiasm unmatched by any other country on Earth. Blocked from expressing their ideas by conventional means, young Iranians swap comments via over 700,000 blogs (web-logs).

At the same time as Iran presents a dour, almost ugly face to the world, with its Soviet-esque new buildings, its black-clad women and its stern-faced mullahs, in private many Iranians share jokes about the extremes of the regime. President Ahmadinejad's insistence that 'Nuclear energy is our irrefutable right!' has become something of an ironic catchphrase behind closed doors in Tehran that can reduce people to fits of giggles. And traditionally Iranians cherished beauty as much as any culture in the world, with a unique reverence for poetry, music, architecture and feminine beauty. The new generation of young Iranians, however, may have more in common with their disenchanted Western counterparts.

Perhaps the apparent contradiction at the heart of modern Iran is a mirror of its extraordinary scenery. At the centre of the country is a vast, almost desert-like high plateau, bone-dry and scorching hot in summer and blasted by icy winds in winter. Nothing could be more puritanical. Yet around it are ranged green hills of gentle beauty and snow-clad mountains of dizzying grandeur. In the north-west, some scholars believe, lay the fabled Garden of Eden. Significantly, Iran has long been fed by crops grown in the dry heartland watered by snows melting in the mountains, channelled through tunnels called *qanats* whose origins are lost in antiquity. Iran's stern heart and lush extravagances have always been mutually dependent.

CHAPTER 2

Iran's Persian Roots

'Welcome, pilgrim, I have been expecting you. Before you lies Cyrus, King of Asia, King of the World. All that is left of me is dust. Do not envy me.'
        Inscription on the tomb of Cyrus the Great
                                at Pasargadae

So much has changed in Iran in recent years that it's easy to forget just how ancient a country it is. Iran's roots are among the oldest of all countries, dating back to the dawn of human civilisation right here in the Middle East. Five or maybe six thousand years ago – long before Stonehenge was even dreamed of – a people called the Elamites settled in the lowlands alongside the Tigris and Euphrates rivers and created Iran's first great cities, including Susa (known today as

Shush), famed in the biblical story of Esther.

The Elamite empire endured well over 2,000 years and saw off first the Sumerians, then the Akkadians, and finally even the Assyrians. Most scholars are in no doubt that there was a huge degree of continuity between the Elamites and the Persians (and modern Iranians) that followed them. Indeed, Susa was the capital of many of the early Persian kings.

The kings of Media

When the Assyrian king Assurbanipal sacked Susa in 646 BC, he was convinced he had finally put an end to the Elamites. Yet although the Elamite empire was gone, other peoples were emerging in the Iran region who would carry on the flame. A wave of Aryan peoples came from the steppe-lands around the Caspian Sea. First were the Medes, who settled in the Zagros mountains and created a capital at Ectabana, modern Hamadan. Under their king Cyaxares, the Medes developed a formidable army. Allying themselves with the Babylonians, the Medes swept down on the Assyrian capital of Nineveh in 612 BC and drove the Assyrians into the abyss of history. By the time he died in 575 BC, Cyaxares had re-established the Elamite empire under the control of the Medes.

Yet following closely on the heels of the Medes was another group of Aryans, the Farsi or Persians, who settled around Fars on the Iranian plateau. Within barely a quarter of a century, the Medes' power was utterly eclipsed by the emergence of a Persian king, Cyrus the Great. Cyrus II was king of the Persian Achaemenes people who would soon give their name to the first Persian imperial dynasty, the Achaemenids. Like Cyaxares, Cyrus built up a large and astonishingly disciplined military machine.

The Achaemenids and the first Persian empire

The turning point for Cyrus was a great victory over his grandfather, the Mede king Astyages. This meant so much to him that the battle-site, Pasargadae, was to be the location of his first capital, and also his tomb. After Pasargadae, Cyrus campaigned far and wide with unbroken success west to Turkey, east into Pakistan and south to Babylon. In just eleven years, he built up the greatest empire the world had yet seen.

Cyrus was not just a brilliant military leader; he was one of ancient history's most remarkable kings. In an age when kingship seemed largely defined by brute force, Cyrus stands out as a beacon of enlightenment with a legendary toler-ance and wisdom.

Cyrus the Great

Cyrus has a reputation for justice and wisdom unmatched in the ancient world. If even half of what is said about him is true, then he set an example of enlight-ened leadership that would be rare even today. The Greek historian Xenophon wrote a book about him called *Cyropaedia*, which Alexander the Great slept with under his pillow (along with Homer's *Iliad* and a dagger).

According to the Roman historian Herodotus, Cyrus promised that he would 'respect the traditions, customs and reli-gions of the nations of my empire and never let any of my governors and subor-dinates look down on or insult them ... I will impose monarchy on no nation. Each is free to accept it, and if any one of them rejects it, I resolve never to reign through war.'

Part of his military success was down to the fact that he was seen in many of the lands he invaded not as a conqueror but a liberator. His conquest of Babylon in 539 BC was typical. When Cyrus rode into Babylon, the people welcomed him with flowers, and in the Bible he is hailed as the messiah who finally set the Jews free from their captivity under the Babylonian kings.

To ensure that the Babylonians were well treated, he famously had these words inscribed on a stone: 'I am Cyrus, King of Babylon, King of Sumer, King of Akkad, king of four countries ... My great army entered Babylon peacefully and I did not allow any harm to come to the land of Babylonia and its people. Babylonians' respectful manner taught me ... and I ordered that all should be free to worship their god with no harm. I ordered that no one's home be destroyed and no one's property taken.'

This stone, called the Cyrus Cylinder,

was discovered in Babylon in 1879 and is now widely regarded as the world's first charter of human rights. In 1971, the United Nations had it translated into all its official languages and put on prominent display in the UN building in New York.

When Iranian human rights campaigner Shirin Ebadi collected her Nobel Peace prize in 2003, she declared: 'I am an Iranian. A descendant of Cyrus the Great. The very emperor who proclaimed at the pinnacle of his power 2,500 years ago "... that he would not reign over the people if they did not wish it", and promised not to force any person to change his religion and faith and guaranteed freedom for all.'

At the heart of Cyrus's attitude, and perhaps his success, may have been the new religion of Zoroastrianism. Although Persian rule is not definitively linked with Zoroastrianism until the time of Darius, the third Persian king, it seems clear that Cyrus was driven by a Zoroastrian vision.

Zoroaster

No one knows exactly who Zoroaster was, or when he lived, but his influence on the emergence of Persia – indeed on the whole of the Western world – was profound. The traditional view is that he was pretty much a contemporary of Cyrus. More recent analysis of the linguistic roots of his poems called *The Gathas* suggests he lived much earlier – maybe around 1700 BC. Russian archaeology puts his date at around 2000 BC. It seems likely that he was a nomadic tribesman living in the north-west of Iran. Some scholars say that his name means 'son of a camel'.

In his famous *Also Sprach Zarathustra* (*Thus Spake Zarathustra*), Nietzsche identifies Zoroaster as the first to divide the world into good and evil – it is this division which Nietzsche wishes to end. Zoroaster's vision was of a world shaped by the battle between light and dark, good and evil. This is not just a cosmic battle between the Supreme God Ahura-Mazda and his evil opponent Ahriman; it's a battle in which every human is free to play his part. According to Zoroaster, we are all 'angels' descended to join the fight against evil and save the world. Yet we are not compelled to join the fight; we have free will. The drawback is that if we don't live well, we will come to grief at the Final Judgement and may be sent to hell. Zoroastrianism is now an almost forgotten religion, practised by people such as the Parsees in India, but it was the root of many key Christian and Islamic ideas.

Zoroastrianism would have told him that Ahura-Mazda, the Supreme God, had entrusted him with the task of uniting the world in one kingdom of justice and peace. It was therefore his sacred duty not only to conquer the world, but to rule over it with tolerance and justice. This concept of justice and just rule – and rule by the consent of the people – has remained at the heart

The value of charisma

In her book *The Iranians*, Sandra Mackey describes how the sign of divine favour, called the *farr*, has been central to Iranian leadership. This quality, which might more prosaically be called charisma, was originally a Zoroastrian idea, but may influence how Iranians think about their leaders even today. In Zoroastrian terms, the idea is that a ruler, like any man, can abandon divine guidance if he wishes. Yet if he does, he loses the *farr*, the divine favour which gives him the right to rule. Thus although a shah was, in theory, divinely chosen, it would be only right to depose him if he lost the signs of divine approval. Several shahs through history lost their thrones when they lost the *farr*, and it could be said that Iran's last shah, Muhammad Reza, lost his throne in 1979 for the same reason.

of Iranian politics until today. Sadly, few of the country's rulers have ever managed to live up to Cyrus's shining example, however.

The Achaemenid kings of Persia who followed Cyrus – including Cambyses, Darius and Xerxes – are all renowned more for their military success, or lack of it, than for championing justice. Of them all, Darius achieved the greatest military conquests, pushing the limits of the empire far across North Africa and into Balkan Europe.

Achaemenid civilisation

Yet the Achaemenid Persian empire was always far more than just an awesome military machine; it was one of the great early civilisations. Linked by paved roads stretching thousands of miles across the empire, it was governed with unusual efficiency and stability by 23 local authorities or satrapies. To communicate across their vast territories, the Achaemenids introduced the world's first postal service, and it was said that relays of horses could deliver mail to the furthest corner of the empire in just a week – faster than any system until the coming of the telegraph in the 1840s.

At the heart of it all was the great city of Persepolis, established by Darius. Persepolis was one of the wonders of the ancient world, comparable to the Egyptian pyramids or the Acropolis, though much less known. What was extraordinary about the Persians was their openness to the best of ideas from outside. Persepolis embodied this to perfection. To build their great city, the Persians gathered the most skilled artists and craftsmen from all the nations of the empire. The result was a multi-cultural concoction that was alone in the ancient world in its mixture of styles. Visitors were awed by its dazzling beauty and sheer size – especially that of the gigantic, multi-columned reception hall.

Persepolis and the first Persian empire met their doom at the hands of the young Macedonian upstart Alexander the Great. Darius's only significant defeat had been in 490 BC when his invading armies were defeated by the Greeks at Marathon – the famous Greek victory that inspired the modern Olympics. Ten years later, the defeat of Darius's son Xerxes by the Greeks at Salamis in Greece marked the start of a long, slow decline in the Achaemenid empire's power. It took well over a century, but by the time Alexander the Great led his armies into the Persian heartland, the Persians were too weak and divided to resist.

The burning of Persepolis

In Christopher Marlowe's great Elizabethan play, *Tamburlaine the Great*, he describes one of the most notorious destructions in history – the burning of the great Persian city of Persepolis by Alexander the Great's victorious troops in a drunken orgy.

Alexander, Thais and the
  Macedonian soldiers,
Reeling with their torches through
  the Persian palaces,
Wrecked to flaring fragments pillared
  Persepolis.

Historians disagree over whether it was simply a wave of drunken looting that simply got out of hand, or an act of political expediency to shock the Persians into submission. For many Iranians, Alexander's name is mud.

The Seleucids and Parthians

On Alexander's death, his vast empire was split between warring dynasties. Eventually, after 42 years, Alexander's cavalry commander Seleucis seized power in Persia, and his Seleucid dynasty ruled for almost 200 years. The Seleucids introduced Greek ideas to Persia, and made Greek the official language. Yet while the elite adopted Greek ways, most Persians held on to their own way of life and nursed their grievances.

Throughout the Seleucid era, trouble bubbled up on the fringes of Persia, and eventually Greek rule was blown away by the Parthians – a tribe of nomads from the Caspian shores who rode their horses and fired arrows with a skill never seen before. Once in Persia, the Parthians settled down and proved remarkably durable rulers, lasting four centuries and bringing to Persian culture such things as a love of painted miniatures and the first flowering of distinctively Persian architecture. Indeed, the Parthians proved so durable that they survived continuous onslaught from the might of the Roman empire.

The Sassanians

Yet the Parthians, too, were foreigners, and like the Seleucids, they never exerted complete control over the kingdom. In the 3rd century AD, Fars, the heartland of Achaemenid power, gave itself its own king, Papak. When Papak's son Ardeshir became king in 208 AD he began to take over more and more of Persia, using a mixture of conquest and diplomacy reminiscent of Cyrus. At last he faced only one rival, the Parthian king Ardavan. When Ardavan challenged him, Ardeshir is said to have replied, 'This throne and this crown were given to me by God' – a claim central to the Persian idea of rulers (see 'The Value of Charisma' above). Ardeshir and Ardavan strode out in front of their armies for a one-to-one combat. Ardeshir slew his rival and so began the Sassanian dynasty, which lasted until the coming of Islam in 637.

Like the Parthians before them, the Sassanians proved a highly resilient dynasty and were, if anything, more successful than the Parthians at keeping the Romans at bay. A famous stone relief at Naqs-i Rustam shows the Roman emperor Valerian in chains after he was captured by King Shapur's troops in 260 AD. Yet, unlike the Parthians, the Sassanians were truly Iranian, and many of the things now associated with Iranian culture appeared in the Sassanian era. The distinctive Islamic domes and vaults are Sassanian ideas, for instance. Persian carpets too had their first great flowering in the Sassanian period, and the first known Persian carpet, the glorious 90-foot square Spring of Khosrow was from a Sassanian palace.

The Magi

Besides dividing the world into good and evil, Zoroaster split man into inner and outer – the flesh and the spirit – and cultivated the idea that man could communicate with God through the spirit. Getting their name from the Magi tribe from ancient Media, magi became the self-appointed guardians of Zoroastrianism, claiming special access to God through their great learning and 'magical' powers. Driven underground by Cyrus and Darius, they became synonymous with occult powers and wizardry, but many were simply scholar priests who studied the world to find signs of God's instructions in things such as star patterns. The most famous of them are, of course, the three Magi who are said to have visited the new-born Christ in Bethlehem.

Zoroastrians prophesied that a bright star would shine in the sky when a saviour was born. On Mount Sistan, according to Iranian folklore, was a temple where three such priests or Magi scanned the sky for such a sign. According to palaeoastronomer Mark Kidger, these priests would have witnessed real astronomical phenomena in 7 and 5 BC – unusual planetary conjunctions followed by the birth of a new star or nova – and set out to Bethlehem with small gifts for the saviour.

The Sassanians adopted Zoroastrianism as the state religion, and for the first time Zoroastrian priests became linked to the king in power and influence. In particular, the magi, the Zoroastrian sages, became closely allied with the throne. That link may have become just a little too close. The splendours and lavishness of the Sassanian court came at a cost to the people of the empire. In time, the Zoroastrians became so tainted by the stench of imperial extravagance that the Iranian people were all too ready to embrace a new religion which offered hope for the poor man, and justice in heaven, if not on earth ...

CHAPTER 3

The Coming of Islam

'Hearken, o ye men, unto my words, and take ye them to heart. Know that every Muslim is a brother unto every other Muslim, and that ye are one brotherhood.'

The Prophet Mohammad

It was in the 7th century AD, after the Sassanids had been in power for over four centuries, that Iran was to gain the other side to its cultural heritage, the coming of Islam, and its effect was, if anything, more profound than the birth of the Persian empire.

As the Sassanian princes reclined on their carpets and cushions in Ctesiphon, the Persian capital, they probably thought little of the effects of their taste for luxuries. Yet across the Persian Gulf, the trade in spices to Persia and Byzantium through the Arabian peninsula was having a hugely disruptive influence on the traditional nomadic Arab way of life. As merchants competed for business in trading towns like Mecca, an uncomfortable social divide opened up between rich and poor. It was in Mecca, of course, that a young spice merchant called Mohammad began to worry about the consequences of the pursuit of wealth.

In 610 AD, when Mohammad was 40, he was sitting one night in the cave beyond the city on Mount Hira where he often retreated. Suddenly, according to the stories, he was startled by a ball of fire. The fiery vision turned out to be the angel Gabriel, who spoke but one word: 'Recite.' Stunned, Mohammad did not react until the angel repeated the command, and he was then blessed with the revelation which later came to be written down as the Koran.

The words of the Prophet

Coming down from the mountain, Mohammad began to preach his message to the people of Mecca to abandon the quest for profit and accept God, Allah, the one all-powerful god. Mohammad quickly found followers among the poor, drawn by his denunciation of wealth and his vision of

THE COMING OF ISLAM • 37

equality for all men. But the wealthy class eventually began to find his ideas too threatening, and in 622 Mohammad was forced to flee Mecca for Medina, an event called the Hegira. By then, however, the rise of Islam as it came to be called (from the Arabic for 'submission' to God) was unstoppable. The appeal of his ideas was such that they swept across Arabia at an astonishing speed, gaining convert after convert. Very soon, Arabia was effectively under the control of Islam.

In 630, Mohammad was able to return to Mecca in triumph at the head of a powerful army of converts. He died two years later, but by then Islam was a massive force. His dying injunction to take the new religion to the rest of mankind was taken up by a ragtag army of Arabs with visionary fervour. They quickly determined to attack the great citadels of wealth.

The Sassanids' downfall

Within barely a year of Mohammad's death, the Arab Muslim army had overrun Syria and then Byzantium, defeating the well-equipped Christian Byzantine army with their sheer ardour and willingness to die in the cause. Within just a few years, they had swept through Persia too and driven the Sassanids to flight. In 638, the Arabs took Ctesiphon and ransacked the Sassanid palaces, destroying their treasures and carrying off the giant Spring of Khosrow carpet to Mecca, where it was cut into pieces.

Although the Persian resistance to the Arab invasion was as bloody and protracted as any they faced, the Arabs triumphed because too many of the Persian people had seen too much corruption and decadence among their rulers – and a taxation burden which had crippled the fringes of the empire. The Persians had lost their faith, too, in a Zoroastrian religion so tainted by its close links with the decadent rule. Indeed, they were all too ready to convert to a new religion which offered more to the poorer man. Many converted out of fear of their Arab invaders, but many more were convinced by Islam's promise of hope.

The Persian conversion to Islam changed the country so quickly and so profoundly that it became the great watershed in the country's long history. Iranian history is either Islamic or pre-Islamic. Islam was originally an Arab religion, of course, and it was an Arab army that drove it into every corner of Persia. Even the Koran was in Arabic. And yet Persian culture proved perhaps more resilient than any other that Islam conquered. Persia became Islamic and took Arabic to heart through the power of the Koran, yet the Persians held on to their language (even though they incorporated Arabic words), and Persian culture and values began to seep their way back into Islamic ideas. Indeed, within a few centuries, Islam had become Persianised, and the great Golden Age of Islam under the Abbasid caliphs of Baghdad in the 8th–11th centuries was in some ways a Persian renaissance.

Persian libraries

It was the very Persianisation of Islam that saved the learning of the great classical writers. After the sack of Rome and the destruction of the library at Alexandria, the tradition of classical learning and the works of Aristotle, Ptolemy and countless others were all but lost to the West, preserved only partially by monks in remote Celtic communities. Yet it was cherished in the massive libraries of Sassanian Persia – until the coming of Islam. The invading Arabs saw these libraries as idolatrous. The caliph Umar issued an edict: 'If the books agree with Islam, then we don't need them. And if they don't, they are *haram*, forbidden.' At once, all the libraries were ransacked and their precious contents burned – all the libraries, that is, but one. In the far south of the Fars region, at Jundi Shapur, a single but well-stocked library survived the purges. Later, a more broad-minded caliph ordered that all the books at Jundi Shapur be translated into Arabic and stored in Baghdad to create the basis for the city's famous Bait al-Hikma, or House of Wisdom. It was from there that they gradually made their way back into the West to inspire the Renaissance. But for the Jundi Shapur library, we would have little knowledge of the great works of classical antiquity – and no Renaissance.

Islam's great schism

Despite its astonishing success, Islam was torn apart almost right from the start by a schism that was to prove every bit as divisive as that between Catholics and Protestants in the Reformation.

When Mohammad died in 632, he left no one as his successor. And the question everyone asked was: just who was his rightful heir?

In Arab society, the succession should go to a male heir. But Mohammad had only a daughter, his beloved Fatimeh, so the patriarchs of the Arab tribes in Mecca and Medina settled on Abu-Bakr as Islam's leader on Earth, or caliph. To avoid confusion, Abu named Umar, part of the old aristocracy of Mecca, as his successor, thus establishing the Umayyad dynasty of caliphs. The multitudes of followers of these caliphs and their descendants would later call themselves Sunnis, from *sunnah*, the tradition.

Yet Fatimeh was married, and so Mohammad had a son-in-law, Ali, and also two grandsons, Hussein and Hassan. What's more, Ali lived an exemplary life. He was self-effacing and peace-loving, which is why he hadn't challenged the nomination of Umar. He also led a very humble life, shunning material possessions. Soon Ali acquired his own set of disciples, later called the Shia'Ali or followers of Ali, who believed that he and his family were the Prophet Mohammad's only legitimate heirs. Meanwhile, the third caliph

Ali and social justice

At the heart of Ali's teaching was a deep concern for social justice, which still resonates through Iranian thinking today. When Iranian clerics charge their leaders with ruling justly, they have Ali's words on their side. Speaking to the governor of Egypt, Ali said: 'You must be just, and the serving of the common man must be one of your prime objectives; the gratification of the aristocracy is insignificant and can be ignored in the face of the happiness of the masses ... Look after the deprived (*mahrum*) and dispossessed (*mustazaf*) who need food and shelter. They deserve your help. Give to them generously from the *bait al-mal* (public fund). It is your duty to protect them and their families.' (Cited in Sandra Mackey's *The Iranians*, from a book by Manocher Doraj, 1990.)

Uthman began to indulge in an ever-more decadent lifestyle, enjoying the fruits of the plunder that the Arab armies had brought back from their conquests. Eventually, resentment among the poor exploded into a slaughterous uprising, and Ali was chosen as the fourth caliph. Five years later, Ali was assassinated, and Uthman's son seized the caliphate and proclaimed his rule over the entire Muslim world.

Shia and Sunni

Since that time there has been an irreconcilable split between Sunni and Shia. The Shia reject all caliphs as usurpers, while the Sunni regard the Shia as dissidents determined to undermine the true religion.

Today, Sunnis are very much in the majority, comprising 90 per cent of all Muslims. The Shia are in the majority only in Iran and southern Iraq.

Shia Islam is very close to the hearts of the Iranian people. Not only was Ali an inspiration with his championship of social justice; Ali's son Hussein drew himself into special alignment with the Persian people. When the last Sassanian princess Shahbanou was captured by Umar's armies, Hussein took her as his bride – thus linking the Prophet's family with the Persian royal family forever. Like Ali, Hussein was an ardent champion of social justice, saying: '[If a man sees a ruler violating the sanctions of God] and does not show zeal against him in word or deed, God would surely cause him to enter his abode in the fire.' No wonder, then, that on many occasions since, Hussein's words have been a rallying call for those Muslims seeking to overthrow unjust rulers.

The tragedy at Karbala

Hussein was very much a man of his word. In 680, Hussein and a tiny band of followers confronted the might of Uthman's army at Karbala in southern Iraq. Although there were only 72 in Hussein's band, facing an army of tens of thousands, Hussein decided to stand his ground. The Umayyad army cut them to pieces, hacking Hussein's head from his body, still proclaiming the word of God.

'Every day is Ashura, every place is Karbala.' Ayatollah Khomeini

As the news of the slaughter at Karbala spread, the waves of anguish that rolled through the Shia'Ali made the split with the Sunni final and irreconcilable. It also gave Shia Islam a sense of martyrdom and pain, and of deep injustice. Every year, at the festival of Ashura, many Iranians in isolated villages still commemorate the death of Hussein with an intense rite in which men dressed in the white of martyrdom beat themselves with chains and hit themselves on the head with swords until the blood flows. Similar emotions of pain and loss, which still bring old people to tears, are created by the traditional *tazieh*, or passion play, which tells the story of Hussein's martyrdom.

Iranian passion play

For those who have witnessed it, the traditional Iranian *tazieh* is an incredibly intense emotional experience. Every year early in *Muharram* (the first month of the Islamic year, around February), in some Iranian villages, the people stage the story of the martyrdom of Hussein. The good characters sing their lines, the bad only speak. Everyone knows the story by heart, yet women watching are drawn into the emotion, weeping at every familiar plot turn as if it were happening there and then. In Terence Ward's book *Searching for Hassan*, he describes how his friend Fatimeh always wept when Sakinah, Hassan's youngest daughter, cries out for water. A young man called Abbas tries to carry a sack of water to her, but his hands are hacked off by the enemy. So he carries the sack to the child in his teeth. The most painful moment in the play, Fatimeh says, is when the orphaned children are left crying in the desert. The famous theatre director Peter Brook describes a *tazieh* he saw like this: 'And when [Hussein] was martyred, the theatre became a truth – there was no difference between past and present ... It was an incarnation; at that particular moment he was being martyred again in front of those villagers.'

While Shia do not believe in caliphs, they do believe in saints and, in particular, saints descended from the Prophet, called imams. Imams are heirs to Ali, and so are the Prophet's mouth-pieces on Earth. Different groups of Shia recognise different numbers of imams. The Lebanese Druze Shia recognise five imams, the Ismailis seven and the Iranian Shia twelve, which is why their brand of Shi'ism is sometimes called Twelver Shi'ism. These twelve passed on the flame one after another between 680 and 873 AD, until the time of the last: Muhammad al-Muntazar, or the Hidden Imam. He is called the Hidden Imam because, fearing for his life, he went into hiding and was never heard of again. He is also the Imam al-Zaman, the Saint of All Time, and it's believed that one day he will come out of hiding as the Mahdi or messiah to restore justice on Earth. Many Iranians pray for his swift return.

CHAPTER 4
Persian Renaissance

'Let not this body live if there is no Iran.'
Words from Ferdowsi's *Shahnameh*, carved
on his tomb near Tus, Iran

Although Iran and Shia Islam are now inextricably linked, it was not always so. It was many centuries after Karbala that a majority of Iranians became Shi'ites, and a thousand years before Shi'ism became the state religion. When Persian culture began to wrest Islam from the Arab Umayyad caliphs in the 8th century, the driving force was a combination of Shia and Sunni. What united them was neither unique religious beliefs nor nationality, but a shared resentment of the ruling Umayyads' extravagance.

As the Umayyad caliphs wallowed in their sumptuous bath-houses and pleasure palaces in

Damascus – furnished by plunder from the nations that Allah's army of the deprived had conquered – discontent began to simmer among those outside the charmed circle of the Arabian aristocracy. Before long, discontent exploded into outright revolt as the followers of yet another branch of Mohammad's family called the Abbasids appeared. Quickly, the Abbasids gathered more and more supporters to their black banner, challenging the Umayyad's white. In January 750, the Umayyad army was utterly routed by the Abbasids on the banks of the Tigris, and the Arab aristocracy was put to flight.

The Abbasid Golden Age

In the hands of Abbasid caliphs, the capital of Islam shifted from Damascus to Baghdad, and the culture of Islam became highly Persianised. The circular layout of Baghdad mirrored that of the classic Sassanian city of Firuzabad. The caliph's court dressed in clothes reminiscent of the Sassanians, and the vast legacy of Persian art, culture and learning was let loose to stimulate what is often called Islam's Golden Age under the Abbasids, which lasted from the 8th to the 11th century. The great works of science and literature compiled in Baghdad's famous House of

Wisdom were all in Arabic, and the famous scholars of the era are described as Arab – Al-Khwarizmi who gave us our modern number system and algebra, Ibn Sina (Avicenna) who wrote one of the world's greatest medical books, and al-Biruni who compared the speeds of light and sound. Yet their scholarship was essentially Persian, and both Al-Khwarizmi and Avicenna were from the old Persian empire, not the Arab world. Al-Khwarizmi was from Uzbekhistan and Avicenna from Bukhara.

Harun and the *Arabian Nights*

The rule of the Abbasids reached its zenith in the time of the caliph Harun al-Rashid and his son al-Mamun. Harun al-Rashid, who became caliph in 786 AD, has become famous for the fictional role given him in *The Thousand and One Nights*, in which the princess Scheherazade staves off her execution by telling tales to the caliph, ending in such tantalising cliffhangers that the caliph just has to keep her alive to hear the next instalment. Of course, the enthralled caliph eventually falls in love with the princess. The stories, which include such famous characters as Aladdin and Sinbad the sailor and Ali Baba, are often called the *Arabian Nights* and are associated with Islam's Golden Age. In fact, they are neither Arabic nor remotely Islamic in origin. The scholar Robert Irwin has traced their roots back to Sassanian Persia, where they were known as *Hazar Afsaneh*; they were compiled for Humai, the daughter of a Sassanian shah, in the ancient Persian tradition of storytelling. When the tales were finally translated into a European language, French, in 1701, their vivid and exotic combination of drama and adventure, romance and comedy captivated audiences, and a whole host of Western writers admitted to being inspired by them, including Poe, Pushkin and Tolstoy.

The rebirth of Persian

The Persian elite quickly adopted Arabic as their first language. Arabic was both the language of court and the language of scholarship. It also had a fluidity of expression that was lacking in the old Persian language of Pahlavi, spoken by most Persians in the time of the Sassanians. Anyone who wrote, wrote in Arabic. Yet most ordinary Persians continued to speak Persian languages, and gradually scholars too began to realise that language was at the heart of Iranian culture. When Ferdowsi composed his great epic poem the *Shahnameh*, he wrote not in Arabic but in Persian, which came to be called Farsi. Just as English became less rigid and formal as it moved from Old English, so did Farsi as it grew out of Old Persian. Indeed, the development of modern Farsi has been likened to the development of modern English, with Farsi adopting many Arabic phrases just as English adopted French. And just as the birth of modern English stimulated a flood of wonderful poetry in the hands of Shakespeare and his contemporaries, so the birth of modern Farsi came with the poetic golden age of Hafez and Rumi (see page 59).

Back in 1786, Sir William Jones, an English linguist, discovered that many of the languages of Europe, the Middle East and India – including English and Farsi – have remarkably similar words for basic terms. The Farsi word for brother, for instance, is *baradur*. Jones realised that all these Indo-European languages had a common mother tongue, sometimes called Aryan, a word from which 'Iranian' comes. Where this mother tongue was first spoken, no one knows. Some scholars say it was on the Russian steppes, some say in Anatolia. It was certainly not far from Iran.

Persian backlash

For 200 years, the Abbasid caliph gave Islam its most graceful and cultivated face – and although Persianised, it was mainly a Sunni face, not Shi'ite. Yet like the Umayyads before them, the Abbasids lost sight of the troubles on the fringes of the empire as they luxuriated in Baghdad. Again, discontent brewed all over the further reaches of Iran. This time Shi'ism began to play a small part. In the 10th century, the Dailamite people of the Elborz mountains in the north of Iran began to build their own empire. Under leaders called the Buyids, they marched south to Baghdad and stormed the city. The Buyids left the caliph in power, but adopted the title Sultan and Shananshah (king of kings) for themselves, reminiscent of the old Sassanian kings. More significantly, perhaps, they established Shi'ite schools in Baghdad and founded the holy Shi'ite city of Qom, where Ayatollah Khomeini first came to fame.

Around the same time, other Persian provinces began to establish their own territories independent of the caliphate. Out to the east into central Asia, the Safavids and Samanids established thriving Persian-style cities – Tashkent, Samarkand and Bukhara – that rivalled Baghdad for culture, learning and architecture. In Kabul, in what is now Afghanistan, Mahmud of Ghazan made a conscious attempt to combine the best of Islam with the best of pre-Islamic Persia – and he enlisted poets and scholars to help him.

The *Shahnameh*

The most famous of the poets enlisted by Mahmud was Abdul Qasim Mansur, better known by his penname of Ferdowsi. Ferdowsi was a Shia Muslim, born in 935 AD in Mashdad in north-eastern Iran. Yet his great poetic work, the *Shahnameh*, focuses on the legends and history of pre-Islamic Persia. The *Shahnameh* is a key symbol of Iranian identity. It's a gigantic work, three times as long as Homer's *Iliad*, yet it means so much to many Iranians that they know great chunks of it by heart. It's a stirring tale featuring many ideas central to the Iranian's self-image – heroism, justice, pride and a sense of inevitable tragedy. At its heart is a deep core of Persian patriotism, and its aim seems to be to separate Persia from Arabia, to find a voice under Islam which means that Iranian culture isn't swamped by Arab culture. It tells stories of the glorious time of a mythical pre-Islamic king called Jamshid, and also of the ultimately tragic defeat of Persia by the Arab army of Islam, which Ferdowsi presents as a national disaster. It's not that Islam is wrong, but that it came with Arab conquest. The lines spoken by a Persian general as he faces the army are well known to many Iranians:

Damn on this World, Damn on this time, Damn on Fate;
That uncivilised Arabs have come to force me to be Muslim.

The Mongol terror

Ironically, just as Persia was beginning to find its own language and identity under Islam, it was beset by a series of terrible and bloody invasions that threatened its very existence. The first and least traumatic was the invasion of the Seljuk Turks in 1045. The Seljuks were more immigrants than conquerors, and even though they took over the reins of power from the Buyids, they often employed Iranian viziers, and did comparatively little damage. The terror came with the next invasion in 1219. This was the year when Genghis Khan's Mongol horde came thundering out of the eastern steppes, wreaking havoc in their path.

After conquering China with astonishing swiftness and ease, Genghis Khan's masses turned their horses westwards. With an army numbering up to 800,000, many with incomparable and ruthless skill on horseback, the Mongols were an unstoppable wave. Bukhara was quickly overwhelmed, and when they reached the university town of Nishapur, the slaughter was dreadful. Every man, woman and child in the city was beheaded, then disembowelled. In other cities that fell in the Mongols' path, people were rounded up and slaughtered for sport like cattle. Those that survived the dreadful onslaught faced years of starvation as the Mongols destroyed the *qanats*, the irrigation tunnels that supplied the fields on the Iranian plateau.

When Genghis's hordes finally tired and withdrew, the Iranians might have sighed with relief.

But the Mongols were not done. In 1256 and 1258, they were back with another horde, this time led by Genghis's grandson Hulagu. Now, even Baghdad wasn't safe. Ignoring the caliph's warning that his death would bring chaos to the world, the Mongols entered the city, killed the caliph and slaughtered perhaps 800,000 people.

No one knows how many Iranians were hacked to death by the Mongols, or how many died of starvation in their bloody wake, but estimates suggest that it was many, many millions. One historian of the time suggested that the blow was so devastating that Iran's population would take a thousand years to recover. He wasn't far wrong. Iran's population finally reached its pre-Mongol level again just a few decades ago.

The terrible slaughter of those years is still etched deep on the Iranian folk memory. Yet there was another dreadful invasion from the east to come in 1384. This was the Tatar army of Tamburlaine the Great, which left a tower of 70,000 heads piled in the square at Isfahan. Ironically, when the slaughter stopped, Tamburlaine presided over the most astonishingly rich flowering of Iranian culture.

The lure of Sufi

The ghastly trauma of the invasions had turned Iranians in on themselves. They hadn't lost their culture. If anything, it had become more precious to them as everything else in life was destroyed. Many Iranians turned to a kind of Islam called Sufism, which emphasised God's love rather than his powers. The Sufis were mystics who relied on their inner resources rather than the material world. At the same time, in a world of destruction, many Iranians wanted to create things of beauty and spirituality.

Tamburlaine was more than happy to cultivate the Iranians' artistic side to decorate his cities, and the Timurid period, as it's called, saw a great flowering of Iranian decoration – including the fabulous faience tiles of Samarkand and exquisite miniatures. Above all, though, the Timurid period saw Iran's poetic Golden Age. Rumi, Jami, Mowlana, Saadi and Hafez all wrote in this period. Rumi and Hafez were both Sufis.

The spread of Shi'ism

For a long while it seemed as if Sufis were content to remain dreamers on the outside of society, distancing themselves from the political

Hafez

Hafez is as important to Iranians as Shakespeare is to the English, and his poetry touches a deep chord. Those few Westerners who know his work testify to his greatness. Goethe said: 'Hafez has no peer.' Lorca spoke of the 'sublime amorous *ghazals* of Hafez', while Emerson described him as 'the prince of Persian poets'. He is most famous for his *ghazals*, short poems of six to fifteen couplets devoted to a particular thought or symbol. What makes Hafez so special to Iranians is his extraordinary humanity and his ability to write about love with clear-eyed candour. He has a unique capacity for finding a universal truth in a small everyday experience. Indeed, many Iranians find his ability to discover the truth so profound that they look to Hafez when seeking guidance. Called 'Divining by Hafez', this involves turning to a Hafez poem at random and seeking the answer in the first lines your eyes settle on.

Hafez lived in Shiraz, and cherished its fine wine and roses. No one drew the link between wine and love with such gentle humour as Hafez. In direct contrast to the puritanical Muslims who followed him, Hafez was immensely tolerant, never accusing the weak, defending the down-trodden and always taking a mischievous generosity to faults in others.

> Do not judge us, you who boast your purity –
> No one will indict you for the faults of others.
> What is it to you whether I am virtuous or a sinner?
> Busy yourself with yourself!

fray. Yet one of the Sufi orders, called the Safavids, began to acquire a large and fervent following as rumours of miracles about them spread. The Safavids were based in Ardabil near Tabriz in what is now Azerbaijan. In the 15th century, the strength of support for the Safavids went to the head of a Safavid leader or sheikh called Junayd, and he began to form an army. His son Haydar built on his work and, realising that Sufi mysticism didn't go hand in hand with getting things done in the real world, he shifted the Safavids towards Shi'ism. When Haydar and his son were killed in 1488, the leadership fell to Haydar's seven-year-old grandson Ismail. The Safavids hurried Ismail away to Gilan on the Caspian Sea. Ismail was a deeply charismatic boy, and with the Safavids' knack for publicity, he came to be widely regarded as the Mahdi, or at least someone who would precede the Mahdi.

At the age of twelve, Ismail emerged from hiding to lead an army of Turkish Shia fanatics, called *qizilbash* (redheads) for their red turbans, and Turkomans from northern Iran. The army moved south through Persia on a holy war for Shi'ism. Soon all of Persia was in Safavid hands, Ismail was made shah, and such was the persuasiveness of the Safavids' evangelism that before long the majority of Persians had converted to Shi'ism. Often their persuasion involved torture, pillage and wholesale slaughter. Yet many became converts because the element of social justice in Shi'ism had a genuine appeal to the long-persecuted Iranians.

Shah Abbas

The Turkish-speaking qizilbash always rubbed along badly with Persian (Farsi)-speaking officials, and over half a century the friction between them rose to ignition point. But just at the point where a conflagration seemed inevitable, in 1588 the Safavid throne came to a brilliant young king called Abbas.

Abbas proved to be the most charismatic and successful of all Persia's rulers since the coming of Islam. He made Shi'ism the state religion and linked it firmly to the ancient Achaemenid notion of kingship, and the connection proved remarkably potent. It seemed to capture the Iranian mindset perfectly, and it gave Iran a national identity it had been lacking for almost a thousand years. Iran was thoroughly Islamic, but it had its own version of Islam, and it had its uniquely Persian legacy too.

Abbas was a shrewd political operator and an inspiring leader. A contemporary of England's Elizabeth I, he became what some scholars describe as Iran's Sun King. With a loyal army of mercenaries, he was able to secure Iran's borders from the threat of the Ottoman Turks to the west, and to stabilise the country internally by

The glories of Isfahan

With its gigantic Imam Square – twice the size of Moscow's Red Square – and its beautiful mosques, Isfahan has long been for many foreign travellers the pinnacle of Persian culture. When English travellers came here in the 1920s, it inspired them to flights of ecstasy. Vita Sackville-West wrote: 'In sixteenth-century Isfahan, Persians were building out of light itself, taking the turquoise from the sky, the green of the spring trees, the yellow of the sun, the brown of the earth, the black of their sheep and turning these into solid light.' In her travel book *The Valleys of the Assassins*, Freya Stark was spurred into even more purple prose. 'The Persian love for the ornaments of life pierces through religion in the domes of Shah Abbas: mistily lost in the blue patterns they melt above our heads like flights of birds into an atmosphere part heaven and part the pale Iranian spring.'

neutralising the qizilbash. He gave Iran what it had long lacked – a national identity distinct from the rest of Islam, and secure borders. In fact, his reign saw Iran become a nation for the first time since the Sassanians – and, as if in celebration, the nation experienced another flowering of art, resulting in perhaps its greatest buildings, including the mosques and square of Isfahan, and the poetry and mathematics of Omar Khayyam.

CHAPTER 5
Persian Twilight?

*'The government of Persia is little else than
the arbitrary exercise of authority by a series
of units in a descending scale from the sover-
eign to the headman of a petty village.'*
British Foreign Secretary Lord Curzon on
Qajar Iran, about 1920

Just as Iranian culture seemed to reach its
apogee under Shah Abbas, and Iran became a
nation for the first time in a thousand years, so
some of the spark seemed to go out. The astonishing vibrancy of Persian culture, art and learning
– a vibrancy sustained right through the Arabic
invasion of Islam, the attacks of the Turks and
the terrors of the Mongol and Tatar hordes –
seemed to dwindle. Of course, it by no means disappeared. But from Abbas's time until the 20th

century, very few artists, craftsmen and thinkers emerged to match those of pre-Abbas times. The architectural glories of Isfahan and Shiraz, the poems of Hafez and Ferdowsi, the great scientific achievements of Al-Khwarizmi and Omar Khayyam – all seemed things of the past.

At the same time, Iran's position in the world seemed to diminish. Once a culture to be admired or feared, depending on your perspective, it had always seemed to be close to the centre of world events. Now it seemed to be becoming something of a backwater, as the world outside changed rapidly, leaving Iran behind. In America and Europe, nations went through industrial, scientific and political revolutions. The Western nations extended their influence across the world – stretching out their power all around Iran, throughout Africa and India and into ancient Iranian territories such as Afghanistan. Yet Iran seemed stuck in the past, unable even to defend its borders when the Ottoman Turks took Tabriz from them in the 18th century – and completely overrun by just 18,000 tribesmen from Afghanistan in 1722. Indeed, the Afghanis pushed Hussein, the last of the Safavid shahs, from the throne and took over the country.

Iran at its nadir

The Afghanis were soon driven from the country by a dynamic soldier of fortune called Nadir Qil Beg, but it was simply replacing one problem with another. Nadir made himself shah and became determined to recreate the Persian empire. With his armies, he stormed into India in 1737, destroyed many of the great monuments of the Moghul empire and carted piles of jewels back to Iran, including the famous bejewelled Peacock throne on which future shahs would sit. The problem was that Nadir was something of a megalomaniac, and he became increasingly brutal in recurring bouts of madness. Thousands of Iranians were murdered for offending Nadir, including many who believed they were his friends. Eventually, after one terror too many, Nadir was assassinated and Iran was plunged into civil war. Stable rule returned only in 1794 when another Turkish group, the Qajars from Mazandaran, muscled their way into power.

Nadir wasn't the first shah of the modern era to brutalise his people, nor the last. The charismatic Abbas, the Iranian Sun King, had in his way been equally tyrannical. In 1615, Abbas had his eldest son murdered. Six years later, he

Protecting the truth

For much of its history, Shi'ism was a dangerous faith to hold. Secrecy was often vital for survival. So Shia theology developed the idea of *taqiyeh*, which could be described as being liberal with the truth to keep the faith safe. If necessary, a Shia, using the idea of *taqiyeh*, could even pretend he was Sunni to avoid danger. Because of the doctrine of *taqiyeh*, Iranian governments have acquired a reputation in the West for sometimes being less than straight-talking. Some commentators say that even Ahmadinejad's attacks on Israel may be an example of *taqiyeh* masking Iran's true attitude.

blinded another of his sons, then another, then his father, and then two brothers. Indeed, Abbas's reign was characterised by the kind of widespread torture and killing of the Shah's opponents that was to become all too commonplace in Iran.

The Qajar shahs

The Qajars proved to be particularly unsatisfactory rulers. Their time as shahs, which spanned the entire 19th century, was one of deep corruption and stagnation in Iran. There was no involvement of the people in government, and all political power rested in the Shah. If, like the Qajar shahs, the leader gave no guidance, then the country drifted. This is exactly what happened in Qajar Iran. As many Western countries dramatically extended their influence around the world in Victorian times, and developed economically and culturally at a tremendous pace, Iran stood virtually motionless. The almost careless suppression of opposition, and massive corruption at every level of government, understandably sapped the will of every Iranian.

The way the tax system worked (or failed to) was symptomatic. The king knew roughly what tax payment he should get from regional governors, but had no idea how they got it. The governors knew roughly what to get from district officers, but had no idea where it came from. And so on, down to the peasant. It was a system guaranteed to breed at best a laissez-faire attitude and at worst wholesale corruption.

To make matters worse, when tax money did reach the Qajar shahs, they simply frittered it away on extravagant living, or buying support with gifts and grand titles – or, in the case of Fath Ali Shah, simply breeding it. Fath Ali Shah spent a fortune on his massive harem of women – so big that he became father to 200 sons. To each of these sons he gave the title Prince, and he sent each one off to be married into an influential family on which he bestowed more titles and more gifts. A common saying of the time was: 'Everywhere in Iran, there are camels, lice and princes.'

When Fath Ali's son Nasir ed-Din, one of the 200, became shah in 1848, he appointed his tutor Amir Kabir as his first minister. Amir Kabir proved to be something of an exception – a leader with genuine drive and vision. He overhauled the administration and built up an efficient army to maintain Iran's borders. He also tried to build bridges with the Shia clerics, and showed energy in dealing with the revolution provoked by the Bahai sect of Islam. But he provoked the wrath of the royal family when he married the Shah's fourteen-year-old sister in 1851, much to her mother's jealous chagrin. Nasir sacked Amir, saying: 'You are a plebeian of humble origin who took [too much] pride in the high positions I provided for you.' He then had Amir taken to a remote location and beheaded.

Britain and Russia

Iran's internal disorganisation and the massive levels of corruption made the country only too ripe a target for Britain and Russia, who were both trying to extend their influence in the region at the other's expense. Britain wanted to safeguard the route to India. Russia wanted a warmwater port on the Persian Gulf. Their hopes for Iran were, of course, mutually exclusive.

Early in the 19th century, Iran lost two wars with Russia – and lost with them Armenia, Georgia and Azerbaijan. It then tried to capture Herat in Afghanistan and was driven away by the British. Thereafter, the British and Russians had no need of military force to get into Iran; the corruption of the shahs provided plenty of openings. To fund their extravagances, the shahs began to sell off the country's resources. Concessions for tax collection, oil production, tea production and much more besides were sold off to British and Russian companies at knock-down prices. Iranians began to seethe at this squandering of the country's assets, and in 1891 Nasir went too far.

Reuters Iran

One of Nasir ed-Din Shah's most notorious sell-offs was his deal with the British Baron Julius de Reuter, the Reuter who set up the news agency. In 1872, for just a tiny sum and a promise of a small royalty payment, Nasir gave Reuter exclusive rights over virtually the entire economy of Iran. Reuter would henceforth have sole control of all the country's industries, all its mineral resources, its future railways and trams, its national bank, and its currency printing. Reuter would even take over Iran's ancient irrigation system. The British Foreign Secretary Lord Curzon later described it as 'the most complete and extraordinary surrender of the entire industrial resources of a kingdom into foreign hands that has probably ever been dreamt of, much less accomplished, in history'. Many Iranians were outraged. Russia was worried about so much going to a British company. Even the British government thought it was a bit much. A year later, Nasir realised his catastrophic error and cancelled the agreement, at great expense.

To fund yet another trip around Europe for him and his huge harem, he granted the British Imperial Tobacco Company the right to buy the entire Iranian tobacco industry for the bargain basement price of just £15,000. Under the agreement, every Iranian farmer had to sell his entire crop to British Imperial at the prices British Imperial set, and every ounce of tobacco smoked would have to be bought at British Imperial outlets.

Iran was then, as now, a country of smokers, with countless people growing small quantities of tobacco on their land, and countless *bazaari* (small shop-owners in the bazaars) selling it. So giving it all over to foreigners was too great an insult for Iranians to bear. Intellectuals, bazaari and farmers were brought together in opposition to the sell-off in a way that Iran had never seen before – and they were joined by the clerics. A great deal of tobacco was grown on land owned by the mullahs, providing income to support the mosques. So for the first time in the modern history of Iran, the mullahs threw themselves into the political fray to challenge the Shah. Amid widespread protest across the country, Sheikh Shirazi, the leading mullah of the day, issued a *fatwa* (religious injunction) on the sale. Nasir had no choice but to back down. It was something of a turning point in Iran's history.

The women of the harem

Harems were part of the Persian ruling class's way of life from the very earliest days of the Achaemenid empire. They survived the coming of Islam, and some of the biggest harems belonged to the Qajar shahs of the 19th century. Westerners have an image of harems as places where beautiful, half-naked girls lie around waiting to serve their master's pleasure. In fact, *harem* is just another word for household, and the harem was simply the area where women and girls lived separately, cut off from the world in their own apartments. Only a few of the women in the Shah's harem were his concubines; the others were all his female relatives and his wives and their relatives. Nasir's harem played a key part in the Tobacco Protest of 1891. Isolated from the private world of the Qajar court, Nasir could ignore the protests of the people, but when the women of the harem, led by his wife Anis al-Dawla, stopped smoking in solidarity, he was forced to take notice. Some scholars believe the Iranian women's movement began in Nasir's harem.

Growing dissent

This challenge to the Shah's authority showed just how far Iranians had felt provoked. Although opposition to the king was suppressed carelessly, it was suppressed brutally. Indeed, the very carelessness made it that much more frightening. Anyone who stepped out of line could be burned, blown from a cannon, buried alive or given the bastinado – hung by his wrists while jailers lashed his feet countless times.

Iran's intellectuals couldn't fail to be aware of how badly this contrasted with so many Western nations – with their protective laws, their parliaments and their liberal constitutions. Even while they felt uncomfortable with Britain's intrusive role in the country, they envied its freedom. Iran's democratic hero of the 1950s, Muhammad Mossadeq – the man who drove the British from Iran – was later to say, when asked where his grandchildren were being educated: 'Why, in England, of course. Where else?' Many Iranians secretly began to read Marx and books about the French revolution.

By themselves, the intellectuals had little power to do much about their hopes for the country. Yet the furore over the tobacco sell-off had sparked a flame. Opposition to the Shah's rule began to spread and connect, as intellectuals, Shia clerics, bazaari and peasants realised that they shared a common enemy in the arbitrary power of the Shah.

Nasir was assassinated in 1896, but his son Muzaffar al-Din proved to be, if anything, worse than his father. In 1900, Muzaffar borrowed 22 million roubles from the Russians to fund a royal trip to Europe. His collateral was Iranian customs receipts. As customs officials began a heavy crackdown to help pay off the loan, Iranians began to take to the streets in protest. When the Shah arrested the agitators, it only inflamed the mood further.

The breaking point came in 1905, when some bazaari in Tehran were arrested for protesting about sugar prices and subjected to the bastinado. The bazaari exploded in protest, and their protest was quickly taken up across the country.

The Constitutional Revolution

The ideas came from the intellectuals, and the energy and finance from the bazaari who saw their livelihoods threatened, but it was the Shia clerics who turned the protest into a revolution. It was only the clerics who could stir up ordinary people, and three clerics in particular – Muhammad Tabatabai, Abdullah Behbahani and Fazlollah Nuri – who held the key to the revolution's success or failure.

With all the opposition united, the widespread protests that flared up in 1905 began to drive the Shah towards concessions. The intellectuals demanded a Western-style constitution to limit the power of the Shah, while the words of Tabatabai echoed from the mosques: 'We want justice, we want a *majlis* [national assembly] in which the Shah and the beggar are equal before the law!'

To keep themselves safe from the Shah's enforcers, thousands of protesters claimed *bast* (sanctuary) inside the garden of the British embassy, and throughout the summer of 1906 kept up the clamour for change. The British embassy garden became a school for revolution, in which people debated the merits of particular forms of government. Eventually, the Shah relented and agreed to both a constitution and the establishment of a majlis. On 7 October 1906, Muzaffar ed-Din Shah presided over the opening of the first Majlis. He had still not signed the constitution, but he was a dying man. Persuaded to do one good thing before he died, the Shah signed, his last act in this life.

It was an extraordinary, historic moment. No Middle Eastern country had ever come anywhere near to achieving constitutional government and equal rights for all its people. Such things had only recently been achieved in many Western countries. Yet here was Iran curtailing the power of the Shah after almost 2,500 years, with only a minimum of bloodshed.

The failure of the Majlis

Unfortunately, this moment of glory was short-lived. The 200-seat Majlis met for the first time on 7 October 1907. Some of the members were directly elected, others put forward by the guilds – butchers, bakers and so on. Yet barely had the first words been spoken in the Majlis than the divisions between the different revolutionary elements appeared. The intellectuals clearly saw the establishment of the constitution as the first step on the road to Western liberal laws. The constitution they created was based on the Belgian constitution of 1831, and they began to introduce European laws and legal terms that had no equivalent in the Shia canon.

Most clerics were at first wary of these foreign introductions and soon downright hostile. It was Fazlollah Nuri who led the attack, and he forced a major concession from the constitutionalists. This was that every law passed by the Majlis would be vetted by a committee of five clerics to see if it was compatible with Islamic precepts, which is why Fazlollah became something of a hero to the 1979 revolutionaries. The new shah, Muhammad Ali, saw his chance to split the Majlis, and his men secretly stirred up protesters

A free press?

The Constitutional Revolution gave new freedom to the press. A whole raft of newspapers appeared for the first time, including *Sur-e Esrafil*, which carried the brilliant political satire of the young Ali Akbar Dehkhoda, the writer who was later to compile the biggest-ever Farsi dictionary. Although numerous papers have been forced to close either by the shahs or the clerics, Iran has always since then had a few newspapers circulating, at least in private, which give a dissident view.

to throng the streets, shouting: 'We want the Koran; we do not want a constitution!' He backed this up with a terror campaign against supporters of the Majlis.

On the 23 June 1908, protesters gathered near the Majlis building in central Tehran and Muhammad Ali seized his moment, sending in Russian-trained troops to round up any dangerous elements. The Majlis building was destroyed, and Tabatabai, Behbahani and many others were sent to jail, while radical preachers like Jahangir Khan were killed.

Those who escaped fled to Tabriz, and for four months held out there. Eventually, the Western powers decided to swing their weight behind the constitutionalists, who marched back towards Tehran, gathering support as they went. This time Muhammad Ali found himself isolated, and fled to the Russian embassy in fear. The constitutionalists took this as a sign of abdication, put his twelve-year-old son Sultan Ahmed on the throne and opened the Majlis again.

Again, though, the Majlis was riven by internal battles as hardline clerics faced off against constitutionalists. Soon, Iranians began to lose some of their faith in the constitution. After just three years, the Shah was able to enlist the aid of 12,000 Russian troops and disband the Majlis again, on pain of death, with apparently only mild murmurs of discontent.

Iran's brief flirtation with democratic government came to be called the Constitutional Revolution. Although in the end it came to nothing, it was by no means forgotten, and the memory of that time sowed seeds of desire in many Iranian minds to have a share in the government of their own country; seeds which were eventually to come to fruition in the Islamic Revolution in 1979, the revolution that ended the age of the shahs once and for all.

CHAPTER 6

The Last Shahs

'Kaar kaar-e engelisaat.' ('The English, of course.')
Iranian joke that the English are at the heart
of every conspiracy, satirised in the novel
My Uncle Napoleon by Iraj Pizishkad, 1973

Iran emerged from the First World War in a weakened and chaotic state. The Majlis was now meeting again, but the infighting between different factions meant that it achieved little, while the Qajar shah Ahmed was young and thoughtless (and grossly overweight). Although Iran was in theory neutral, Russia, the Ottomans and the British had occupied it at will during the war. Indeed, if Russia hadn't been busy with its revolution, the country would probably have gone the same way as Georgia and Azerbaijan and become just another part of the Soviet empire. The economy had all but collapsed, tax revenues had dried to a trickle and the bankrupt government was reduced to paying civil servants in bricks.

It was into this mess that stepped the man who at first appeared to be Iran's saviour, Reza Khan. Reza Khan was a giant of a man from the Elborz mountains with a savage temper and an iron will, who gained the nickname 'Machine Gun Reza' in the Cossack Division, the troop originally trained by the Russians to protect the Shah. Despite his fearsome reputation, he was just a mid-ranking officer until 1921, when the Caspian Sea province of Gilan, inspired by the Russian revolution, decided to break away from Iran. The Iranian government hesitated, uncertain what to do.

The Cossack's coup

Reza Khan had no such uncertainty. It was clear that the country needed pulling into line, and Reza Khan believed he was just the man to do it. Perhaps encouraged by the British, he took control of the Cossack Division and headed south from Qazvin where he was stationed. At midnight on 21 February 1921, he led his 3,000-strong troop into Tehran and arrested the entire

Iranian cabinet. Reza Khan demanded that the Shah put him in charge of the whole army, and appoint his supporters as ministers. The Shah had little choice but to agree.

Schooled by his long years in the Cossacks, Reza Khan was convinced that the only way to restore Iran's national stability and pride was with military discipline. He quickly trained up an army and stormed out across the country to bring all the shaky elements into line. In December 1921, he drove the Bolsheviks out of Gilan and crushed the rebellion. A few months later, he stamped out rebellions in Azerbaijan and Khorasan. By the middle of 1923, he had brought the Kurds in the north-west and the Qashqai and Bakhtiari tribes in the south under his iron heel. The Russians realised that they had too much on their hands to pressurise Iran any more, while the British were only too pleased to see a strong presence in Iran to keep the Russians at bay. Suddenly, Iran seemed strong and independent again, and Reza Khan became something of a hero.

Meanwhile, the obese Shah had gone abroad, ostensibly for medical treatment, but it seemed unlikely that he would return. The Iranian press urged Reza Khan to lead the country as president of a republic. Yet the mullahs were incensed, fearing that getting rid of the Shah would make way for the same attacks on religion that neighbouring Turkey was seeing under Kemal Ataturk's new republic. Yet it was clear that Reza Khan was in control of the country, so the mullahs summoned him to Qom and suggested that he become Shah instead. Reza Khan agreed, and on 31 October 1925, Ahmed Shah was officially deposed and Reza Khan became Reza Shah, the first king of the Pahlavi dynasty.

The Pahlavi shah

It was an extraordinary moment for a man of humble origins who could neither read nor write. Yet, unlike every shah since the coming of Islam, he spoke Farsi, the language of his people. For some, it was as if the king in hiding had finally come into his own in the country's hour of need. People in Tehran hung out flowers and carpets to greet the new shah.

Reza Shah led the country in the same stern-handed way as he had led the Cossacks, and treated his subjects as he had treated his subordinates. The country he inherited was in a parlous state. While European cities had motorways, skyscrapers, underground systems and airports,

Tehran was still much like a medieval village, full of crumbling mud buildings and narrow streets suitable only for camels and donkeys. Reza Shah was convinced that if he could modernise the country, it could at last stand proud on its own two feet among the great nations of the world. So he embarked on a modernisation programme with a zeal that would have put both the Communists and the Nazis to shame.

Razing Iran

Huge areas of old buildings were torn down in Tehran, Tabriz and Shiraz to make way for concrete apartment blocks and wide, straight streets suitable for cars and trucks. Troops were deployed to plant trees with the order: 'If the tree dies, you die.' Motor roads were built, factories established, and – most importantly of all for Reza Shah – Iran's first railway was built. Linking the Persian Gulf to the Caspian Sea, this 865-mile railway was an extraordinary engineering feat, but the drain on the country's resources was enormous.

Meanwhile, rural areas were forced through equally dramatic changes. Reza Shah was convinced that the nomadic way of life of the many ancient Iranian tribes – the Qashqai, Baluchi, Bakhtiari, Lur and many others – was outmoded.

THE LAST SHAHS • 89

Impatient for change, he sent soldiers out to force these nomads into villages at gunpoint, taking away their herds and insisting that they learned to farm. Ways of life dating back thousands of years were shattered in a few years, and tribesmen living in cramped conditions in unhealthy villages, unused to farming, died in huge numbers.

Cut-throat Reza

Reza Shah was extraordinarily ruthless in his quest for improvement. Once, on a visit to Hamadan in western Iran, for instance, he found that people were going hungry because bakers were hoarding wheat to drive up prices. Reza Shah had the first baker he saw thrown in an oven and burned alive. Next day, the shops were filled with cheap bread.

It wasn't simply the economy and infrastructure that Reza Shah wanted to modernise. He wanted to yank the country's entire way of life into the 20th century. He made education compulsory for all Iranians, boys and girls. He created the University of Tehran. He instigated a public health system. He put the law on a more rational, Western footing – leaving Islamic Shari'ah law to cover only minor matters such as marriage.

Attacking Islam

All the time, he knew his biggest obstacle to progress was Shia Islam, and with his characteristic ruthlessness he aimed to cut the mullahs down to size. First of all, he emphasised the pre-Islamic side of Persian culture. He renamed the country Iran, as it had been called in Cyrus's time. He instructed architects to draw their inspiration from the Achaemenid style, even when building such things as police stations and banks. And he insisted that every Iranian child should learn parts of Ferdowsi's *Shahnameh* by heart. Parents were encouraged to give their children old Iranian, not Islamic names.

At the same time, he curtailed the power of the mullahs in law, by making it compulsory for every lawyer to complete a secular law degree. And he confiscated the mullahs' land to pay for all his modernisations.

Most notoriously of all, he confronted Islam

over its attitude to women. He insisted that by keeping women at home, Iran was losing half its workforce. He encouraged girls to go to university – and he made it illegal for cinemas, restaurants and hotels to bar women as they had before. Most shockingly of all, he made it illegal to wear the chador (the veil) in public. While some women found the removal of the chador a hugely liberating experience, many found it humiliating, as if they were being forced to walk naked in public. Rather than face such degradation, many stayed at home.

Reza's downfall

Throughout these dramatic upheavals, most Iranians – even the mullahs – kept quiet. Some people genuinely welcomed the changes. Others thought it was the price that had to be paid for a strong, independent Iran. Many more were simply too terrified of Reza Shah to resist. In 1936, a crowd gathered inside the Imam Reza mosque in Mashdad to protest against Reza Shah's attacks on Shi'ism. Soldiers were sent into the mosque, where they went up into the gallery and fired machine guns into crowd, killing anywhere between 100 and 400 people.

It was not the Iranians who finally got rid of

Reza Shah; it was the British and Russians. To keep these two powers out, Reza Shah had forged links with Nazi Germany – and his whole regime smacked of fascism. Indeed, he was outspoken in his support of Hitler. When the Second World War broke out, Russia and Britain found themselves on the same side, and Reza Shah found himself branded a Nazi collaborator. Suddenly up against the entire Allied might, the Shah's tough army seemed tiny. As British and Russian troops converged on Tehran in 1941 with a view to using the national railway as a vital supply line to Russia, Reza Shah found himself isolated. He abdicated and fled the country, while the British put his playboy son Muhammad Reza on the throne. Those tribesmen still alive destroyed their hated villages and headed back to their old herding grounds.

Lacking the steel of his father, and the support, Muhammad Reza trod a very cautious path after the war. He allowed the wearing of the chador again, returned many of the mullahs' confiscated lands, and set free many political prisoners. Outside, things seemed quiet too. Russia was too exhausted by the war, and Britain had lost some of its interest in Iran with the independence of India. However, the Americans, dominant in the world after the war, were now taking a keener interest instead – enough for Norman Schwarzkopf (the father of 'Stormin' Norman' of Gulf War fame) to be brought in to train the Shah's police. And Britain still had one very significant interest in Iran – oil.

CHAPTER 7

An American Coup

'You do not know how evil they [the British]
are. You do not know how they sully every-
thing they touch.'
Iranian prime minister Muhammad Mossadeq
to US diplomat Averell Harriman, 1952

The event that has most deeply coloured Iran's
relationship with the West over the last half-
century began in 1901. That year, in one of the
most notorious of the Qajar shahs' foreign sell-
offs, Muzaffar ed-Din had given British financier
William Knox D'Arcy sole rights to Iran's oil
reserves for the next 60 years. No one knew just
what those reserves were, but as D'Arcy had
guessed, they turned out to be stupendous. Before
long, the Anglo-Iranian Oil Company (AIOC) was
pumping up huge quantities of oil from the rocks

beneath Khuzestan in southern Iran. The British government took a 51 per cent share in the company.

The battle over oil

Winston Churchill later described Iranian oil as 'a prize from fairyland beyond our wildest dreams'. It was Iranian oil that kept British warships steaming through two world wars and supplied 90 per cent of Europe's oil in the immediate post-wars. At Abadan near the Iraq border, AIOC (later known as British Petroleum, BP) built what was, until 1980, the biggest oil refinery in the world.

By 1950, Iranian oil was the prime energy source of much of the Western world – and yet Iran was getting peanuts for it. That year, Iran received a total of $45 million; the UK exchequer got $142 million from the tax on AIOC's profits alone. To make matters worse, AIOC treated its Iranian employees shabbily. When the workers went on strike in protest in 1946, AIOC instigated a riot which left dozens dead.

The rise of Mossadeq

For Iranians, AIOC began to become a symbol of their humiliation and exploitation by the British.

Ironically, it was the British expulsion of the tyrannical Reza Shah that finally opened the way for the expression of Iranian resentment. With Reza Shah gone, the Majlis, long quiescent, began at last to find a voice, and the focus of much of their anger was British oil.

Leading the attack was Muhammad Mossadeq. Mossadeq was one of the few members of the Majlis who had stood against Reza Shah's accession to the kingship – and he had paid for his opposition by exile from politics. But now he was back, with all the kudos of a martyr. Although almost 70, Mossadeq was incisive, gracious and a brilliant political operator.

As the demands for a better deal began to emerge from Iran in the late 1940s, AIOC grudgingly entered negotiations. Convinced that they had the upper hand, the British began to lean on the Shah to keep the Majlis in line, reminding him that he owed them his throne. At first, he was too timid to know what to do. Then in February 1949, a young man stepped out of a crowd and shot Muhammad Reza. Five shots were fired from close range, yet remarkably only one hit the Shah, just grazing his cheek. For the Shah, his survival was a revelation. Clearly he was destined to rule. At once he went into action, banning left-wing organisations like the Tudeh and sending out his hit squads of police to round them up. Then he ordered the creation of a second house, the Senate, to put a check on the rising power of the Majlis – knowing that he would choose over half the senators personally. Finally, he seized from the Majlis the power to appoint the prime minister. But events were soon to spiral beyond his control.

AIOC managed come up with a paltry improvement to their existing deal, and began to pressurise the Shah to get it agreed by the Majlis. The Majlis, anxious not to provoke a backlash, simply stalled until the time came for the next elections. The Shah was determined to bring the Majlis to heel, and so blatantly rigged the vote that none of AIOC's opponents, not even Mossadeq, was elected.

This was too much for the Iranian people. Riots broke out across Tehran and many other cities in protest. Then Mossadeq led a huge band of protesters to the palace gates and declared that he wouldn't move until free and fair elections were held. The Shah reluctantly agreed.

The National Front

Opponents of AIOC decided to put aside their differences and form the National Front, the first popular party in Iran's history. Mossadeq, of course, was to be the leader. He was by now a hugely popular figure, mobbed by supporters when he walked through the streets.

Many clerics hated the possibility that the National Front might champion secular laws and democracy that went against Shari'ah law. Yet they hated the power of infidel foreigners over Iran even more. Soon Mossadeq was joined by a group of clerics led by the charismatic Ayatollah Kashani, whose political activism later proved to be the inspiration for Ayatollah Khomeini.

The combination of the National Front and the clerics in the newly-elected Majlis proved to be a powerful one. Mossadeq was at once put on the committee to look at the oil deal, where he very much controlled the tone with his acerbic comments. The British were now getting worried. They sent warships to the Gulf and instructed the Shah to appoint the no-nonsense General Ali Razmara as prime minister to push the AIOC's 'compromise' deal through. But within a few days Razmara was dead – shot, apparently, by another young fanatic.

The Majlis assembled on 15 March 1951 to debate another of the Shah's British-prompted nominations for prime minister. To everyone's

The few

Many outsiders believed that it was the 'block-headed British' who pushed the Iran oil situation to crisis point. People like President Truman's Secretary of State Dean Acheson believed that if AIOC had been willing to give just one inch, a compromise could have been found. It was their very belligerence and old colonial bluster that undermined Iranians like Razmara and brought Mossadeq to power. Yet, when Winston Churchill was elected PM again in 1952, the British stance became even more inflexible. In a parody of Churchill's most famous saying, Acheson commented: 'Never had so few lost so much so stupidly so fast.'

surprise, Mossadeq kept silent. Then a British-paid deputy, Jamal Emami, began to taunt Mossadeq, saying he hadn't the guts to offer anything positive. As Emami sat down, Mossadeq, in a brilliant piece of political theatre, quietly stood up and thanked Emami for his invitation to become prime minister, which he accepted with humility. The Majlis cheered. It was put to the vote, and Mossadeq's nomination was approved with a huge majority. Instantly, Mossadeq said he could serve as PM only if the Majlis agreed to complete nationalisation of AIOC. Approval was unanimous. The unthinkable had happened.

British reaction

The British were completely flabbergasted at this act of defiance. Cries of outrage rang across the British Foreign Office. Iranians, exhilarated at their daring, began to wonder if the British might invade, as warships moved up the Gulf. British Prime Minister Clement Attlee, pushing through Britain's own nationalisations at the time, thought of compromise. But Foreign Secretary Herbert Morrison warned him that it would set a terrible precedent – and so Britain went on collision course with Iran.

By now Mossadeq was a national hero, and it was clear that it was he who was leading the country, not the Shah. For the first time, the British couldn't simply pull strings to get what they wanted. Uncertain what to do, they called all their British staff home – not before subtly sabotaging equipment to ensure that it would soon begin to fail. At the same time, they set up a blockade on all oil exports from Iran, insisting that any oil the Iranians tried to sell was stolen goods.

'Mossy' in America

In 1951, Mossadeq went to America to put his case against the British in front of the United Nations. His style, elegance and wit, combined with his obvious frailty and theatricality, made him something of a celebrity there. In fact, *Time* magazine made him their Man of the Year. While the British establishment regarded him as a hysterical, slippery, wily, absurd Oriental, the Americans found him much more appealing. When it came to his performance at the UN, the British had expected him to cave in before the eloquence of the British spokesman, Sir Gladwyn Jebb. In fact, Mossadeq was more than a match for him, and Britain's resolution to condemn Iran was humiliatingly thrown out.

Britain tried to cajole the Americans into joining them in their tough stand against Mossadeq. While President Truman was in power, the Americans were willing to act only as brokers to negotiate a deal. But once Eisenhower came to power in 1952, the American attitude changed, and they began to see an out-of-control Iran as a weak spot in their fight to contain Communism. Indeed, the very day Eisenhower came to power, he agreed to a CIA plan to get rid of Mossadeq. The plan, called Operation Ajax, was to be the first CIA coup.

Bedside diplomacy

Mossadeq was an old man. He suffered from ulcers, and often seemed unable to walk without a cane. He also tended to fall in a faint every now and then. Yet no one knew just how frail he was, since at times he seemed able to move about with remarkable agility, and his faints seemed sometimes to occur at very opportune moments politically. Most extraordinarily, during the height of the oil crisis when he was leading the country, he often retired to his bed, and held meetings there in his pyjamas with everyone including the American Secretary of State, looking all the while at death's door but negotiating with steely determination.

Kermit's coup

In a scenario brilliantly described in Stephen Kinzer's book *All the Shah's Men*, Kermit Roosevelt, grandson of Theodore Roosevelt, established a CIA team in a rented villa in Tehran, and then in the American embassy. Once in place, Roosevelt began doling out millions of dollars to buy support in the right places – clerics, army officers, politicians and, of course, the press. One CIA operative believed that 80 per cent of the press soon came under CIA control. Articles written by the CIA condemning Mossadeq as a mad fanatic would be splashed across all the national newspapers. There was cash, too, for thugs and lowlife, such as the infamous Shaban the Brainless, willing to stir up trouble and start riots targeted at Mossadeq. Even Ayatollah Kashani was persuaded to turn against Mossadeq with a wad of CIA cash.

Iranians accepted that they might have to go through some pain to get rid of the British, but the oil embargo began to have a catastrophic effect on the economy, and the soon daily riots and the non-stop attacks on Mossadeq began to take their toll. Mossadeq wondered if he should step down. Roosevelt decided it was time to put his machine in motion.

Roosevelt's first coup attempt failed, and the Shah, fearing that he would be blamed, fled to Rome. But on 19 August 1953, Roosevelt launched a second coup. This time the Americans, claiming that they were worried about damage to property, duped Mossadeq into sending the police in hard against the rioters. But most of the police were royalists and, once unleashed, encouraged the rioters to turn on Mossadeq, who was forced to escape from his house by climbing over the back wall.

At once, the CIA's tame General Zahedi was declared prime minister, using a diktat obtained earlier from the Shah, and the army and police took over. Unaware of events, Muhammad Reza Shah was sitting dejectedly in his Rome hotel when a group of journalists burst in with the news that Mossadeq had been deposed. Once the shock had sunk in, he jumped up, shouting 'I knew it! I knew it! They love me!', and set about the preparations for his triumphant return.

The 1953 coup: the verdict

Kermit Roosevelt and many others firmly believed that the 1953 coup was absolutely necessary. Without it, they felt that events in Iran might have spiralled out of control. At best, Iran might have fallen into the hands of the Communists. At worst, it might have drawn the world powers into a conflagration leading to the Third World War. For just a few million dollars, they felt, they had solved a crisis and brought stability to the region. In fact, the CIA was so cock-a-hoop with the success of their coup that they went on to instigate a string of others, from Guatemala to Chile. Yet now there's a growing consensus among historians of the time that the Iran coup may turn out to be the biggest mistake that the USA made in the 20th century.

First of all, it gave Muhammad Reza Shah the chance to become a dictator – and his tyrannical rule drove Iranians to the point of despair. In 1979, their anger erupted in the Islamic Revolution. Although most Americans quickly forgot their role in the coup, Iranians did not. From that time on, America's image in Iran turned blacker and blacker until it came to be regarded as the Great Satan. When Americans were taken hostage in the Tehran embassy siege in 1979, several of the hostage-takers were survivors from the 1953 National Front. The Americans' perfidy burned strong in their memories.

Ironically, the 1953 coup turned a country on the verge of becoming the Middle East's first mature democracy into a hotbed of resentment. Once they learned the truth, as they did quite soon, most Iranians were incensed by the way the USA had opened the door for the return of a vile dictator. And that resentment, in turn, opened the door for the growth of extremism in Iran – partly because all other avenues seemed useless. Many commentators are certain that it was the 1953 coup that planted the seeds of today's Islamic terrorism and Iran's aggressive stance in the world. Ayatollah Khamenei, Iran's current Supreme Leader, has said defiantly: 'We are not liberals like Allende and Mossadeq, whom the USA can snuff out!'

CHAPTER 8

The Islamic Revolution

'All of Islam is politics.'

Ayatollah Khomeini

As Mohammed Reza Shah and his new American friends celebrated their successful overthrow of Mossadeq and the Nationalist movement, they little imagined that they were setting off down the road that would lead to the third great Iranian upheaval of the 20th century, the Islamic Revolution of 1979. But the fire of resentment against oppression that the coup had stamped out was left smouldering beneath the surface, and would eventually burst forth as a raging inferno.

The White Revolution

Egged on by the Americans, the Shah decided to follow in his father's footsteps and push the country towards modernity in what came to be called the White Revolution. Although it included government reorganisation, privatisation and emancipating women, the central plank of the Shah's grand scheme was land reform. In 1963, 75 per cent of Iranians were still peasants, and just a few hundred people owned 85 per cent of the land. Muhammad Reza decided to take the large landholdings of the aristocracy and the clerics and redistribute them among the peasants.

It seemed like a laudable idea to Westerners, but the whole thing, in fact, was ill-thought through and turned into a disaster. Stripped of the feudal landlords who had maintained them, irrigation networks collapsed, leaving villages struggling for survival. As fields turned to dust, many newly landed peasants simply sold up and headed for Tehran. Agribusiness and mechanised farming moved in to take their place, but soon began to grind to a halt as imported machinery broke down in the fields, with no spare parts to repair them. By the mid-1970s, for the first time in its history, Iran could no longer feed itself. Prices went through the roof as food was imported from abroad and inflation ran rampant, making people's hard-won savings worthless overnight. As the rural poor massed in the shanties of southern Tehran, resentment began to simmer.

Cocooned in Golestan Palace, the Shah seemed oblivious to this. The world oil crisis in the early 1970s gave Iran a cash bonanza as oil prices skyrocketed. The Shah and his friends were able to live the high life. The West praised him for his reforms, and Western magazines featured his beautiful wife and lavish lifestyle. Americans poured in to join the party, and neon signs flashed as Coca-Cola and Pepsi battled it out for the tastebuds of the teenage offspring of the new rich. But all too little of this filtered down to the poor, who saw rich foreigners revelling in their Persian lifestyle and fat-cat Iranians spending their cash on foreign luxuries.

Military muscle

Maybe the Shah was aware of the dangers. His efforts to suppress dissent bordered on paranoia, and his regime became as oppressive and tyrannical as any in Iran's history. Everywhere Iranians went, there were members of the security forces watching them. All too visible were watchtowers and machine gun posts along main roads. Less visible, but even more frightening, was Iran's

KGB, SAVAK, which whisked dissenters away in the night to imprisonment and torture, and which was rumoured to poison those who went too far in their criticism of the Shah.

Persian extravaganza

In an effort to counter-balance the power of Islam, Muhammad Reza Shah promoted the glories of pre-Islamic Persia, and the continuity of rule from the days of Cyrus the Great. By a little bending of the facts, 1971 could be celebrated as the 2,500th anniversary of the creation of the first Persian empire. So the Shah decided to commemorate it with a huge extravaganza at the ruins of Persepolis. The Shah decided that no expense should be spared, and the cost escalated to $300 million. Unfortunately, this extravaganza, which turned out to be more Hollywood B-movie than ancient glory, was open only to the elite in Iran and to the Shah's Western allies. To add to the insult, nearly all the materials and props were made, not in Iran by local craftsmen, but by factories in Europe and America. Worse still, the event coincided with a summer in which drought brought famine and hardship to many people in the south around Persepolis. Even before the event started there were violent protests, with opponents claiming that the Shah was detaching himself from Islam. Rather than improving the Shah's standing by associating him with Persia's glories, it simply confirmed him as a jumped-up autocrat, frittering away the country's resources while ordinary Iranians suffered.

Meanwhile, the Shah used oil revenues to modernise the army – and the Americans were only too ready to supply him with all the latest military hardware. They were even happy when the Shah began to embark on a nuclear power programme.

But opposition to the Shah was beginning to boil beneath the surface. In the 1960s, radical writers like Jalal Al-e Ahmad attacked the

Westernisation of Iran, which he saw as the root of its problems. Al-e Ahmad coined the famous term *gharbzadegi*, or Euromania. Westernised Iranians, he argued, suffered from a disease called occidentosis. 'An occidentotic who is a member of the nation's leadership is standing on thin air; he is like a particle of dust suspended in the void … He has severed his ties with the depths of society, culture and tradition.'

By the 1970s, most secular opposition to the Shah and Westernisation, though, had been suppressed. All dissident political parties and meetings were banned, newspapers were essentially the tools of the Shah's friends, and publishing houses failed to publish any of the 'wrong' books. Al-e Ahmad was rumoured to have been poisoned by SAVAK.

The voice of Islam

Yet there was one voice that could not be silenced – that of the clergy. As the mullahs preached in the mosques every week, they could spread ideas to the mass of ordinary people right across Iran. With no other outlet for their frustration, many Iranians turned to religion for solace. Moreover, the clergy had one especially powerful and outspoken figurehead, Ayatollah Khomeini.

Traditionally, the clergy had held themselves aloof from politics, but Khomeini, taking his cue from clerics like Ayatollah Kashani, argued that it was a Muslim's duty to attack the Shah if he was seen to be going against Allah's will.

The Shia clergy

The Shia clergy are known as mullahs, though in Iran this is almost a slang term. In Islam, there's no such thing as ordination, but mullahs join the *ulama* or community of scholars. Until Reza Shah's time, almost anyone could grow a beard and wrap on a turban and call himself a mullah. Now mullahs have to train as *talebeh* (students) at a recognised place, most importantly in the *madreseh* or colleges at Qom, Iran's theological centre. From Qom, some mullahs go out to become village priests. The more gifted scholars stay on for years of hard study to become a *mujtahid* or jurist. Unlike ordinary people, mujtahids have the right to interpret Shari'ah law. In contrast to

Sunni Muslims who take the Koran as the complete, unalterable truth, Shia believe that it may be interpreted and redefined by the right kind of reasoning. Mujtahids are the only people equipped to make such interpretations. The best mujtahids are dubbed by their peers *hojjat ol-eslam*. The very best are called *ayatollahs*. Ayatollahs are never officially appointed; it's simply generally recognised when they have reached this status. A very rare ayatollah may be called *marja-e taqlid*.

Who was Ayatollah Khomeini?

The man who was to become the spear-head of Iran's Islamic Revolution was born Ruhollah in 1902 in a modest mud-brick house in the village of Khomein in central Iran. The name Khomeini was a later acquisition. When he was just an infant, Khomeini's father was murdered in revenge by the friend of a man he had executed for not fasting one day in the month of Ramadan. Khomeini grew up a determined and relentless pursuer of justice. He studied the Koran and went to Qom to become a mullah. A very gifted scholar, he made his way right through the hierarchy to become an ayatollah. He became a mullah in the same year as Reza Khan became Shah, and watched his Westernisation with increasing concern, which he expressed in his book *Secrets Exposed* in 1944. He kept out of politics, though, until 1961, when his superior Ayatollah Borujerdi died. Borujerdi felt that clerics had no business indulging in politics; Khomeini had no such qualms. After Borujerdi died, Khomeini felt free to launch himself into politics with a force and determination that no mullah had ever shown before. Breaking centuries-old tradition, Khomeini argued that it was a mullah's duty to oppose the Shah if the Shah was wrong.

In 1962, Khomeini launched a blistering attack on the land reforms from the theological centre at Qom. By depriving the clergy of their lands, the reforms were, he insisted, an assault on Islam itself. In retaliation, the Shah sent his troops into Qom. They arrested scores of theological students, and killed two as they stood there with their Korans. At the students' funeral, Khomeini hurled condemnation at the Shah, calling him a miserable wretch and proclaiming: 'The nation will not allow you to continue this way!' When Khomeini was arrested, mass rioting spread across Iran in which 86 people died; 7,000 troops were called out to suppress it.

After his release, Khomeini carried on his verbal tirades undaunted. In 1964, he launched an assault on the government's plan to give American soldiers immunity from prosecution. This, he thundered, reduced the Iranian people to a level lower than that of an American dog, since if anyone in America ran over a dog they would be prosecuted for it, while if an American ran over an Iranian he would be immune. The Shah instantly banished Khomeini, who settled at Najaf in Iraq. Here, far from being quietened, he hurled ever more strident and damning indictments at the Shah, gaining all the charisma of

Ali, driven into the wilderness by the Umayyad caliphs.

The supreme spiritual guide

In 1963, Khomeini delivered a series of crucial lectures laying out an idea called the *Velayat-e Faqih*. For over a thousand years, Shias had passionately believed that all government since the disappearance of the Hidden Imam was profane – which is why mullahs never stooped to politics. Khomeini insisted that divine will permits neither injustice nor ungodly rule. Until the Hidden Imam reappears, Khomeini argued, it is the duty of Shia jurists to lead the people. 'Kingship', he said, 'has been the shame of history, from the day it started to this very day.' The only legitimate rule would be by one supreme, just jurist or *faqih*, like Ali when he was caliph. Later, Khomeini himself would be Iran's first *faqih* since Ali.

The road to ruin

Meanwhile, the mid-1970s saw world oil prices collapse, and suddenly the oil wealth that had been flooding into the country began to dry up. As the economy went from bad to worse, conditions among the poor began to get desperate, while even the middle class were having their lives torn apart by rampant inflation. And still the Shah's conspicuous consumption went on.

In January 1978, the newspaper *Ettelaat* ran an article accusing Khomeini of being a homosexual. Students in Qom gathered to protest, and when they refused to disperse, the police gunned them down, killing twenty.

Massive street demonstrations and sabotage began to erupt in the streets of Iran's cities, and more and more people called for the Shah to go. In the universities, students demanded democratic reforms, and girls put the chador on over their jeans. In the shanties, huge masses of ordinary people gathered to voice their anger. And in the mosques, clerics across the land urged resistance, citing the example of Karbala again and again.

Increasingly desperate to hold up his tottering regime, the Shah began to resort to more and more brutal tactics. Thousands of demonstrators were killed as soldiers opened fire in street battles in Tehran, Qom and Tabriz. SAVAK hunted down ringleaders mercilessly. Then in August 1978 they went too far. Apparently, so rumour said, when SAVAK chased militants into a cinema in Abadan, they managed to set it on fire – and 400 women and children trapped inside were burned to death. Many who had remained neutral now came out on the side of the revolutionaries.

The Shah's final moments

As the protests mounted, the Shah's army began to panic. On 8 September, they fired randomly into a crowd of demonstrators in Tehran, killing scores and leaving the pavements running with blood. With this 'Black Friday', the last vestiges of support for the Shah evaporated. The desperate Shah leaned on Saddam Hussein to force Khomeini out of Iraq. Khomeini went to Paris, where, with the world's press at his door and modern communications at his disposal, he began to mount a relentless campaign.

Now, at last, the masses of ordinary people who had stood aside during the Constitutional Revolution and the Nationalist movement joined in the demonstrations and the protests. The Shah tried imposing a curfew, but the trickle of soldiers deserting the army had now become a flood, and soon the Shah had no one to impose it. Early in January 1979, more than two million people surged through the streets of Tehran, shouting: 'God is great, Khomeini is our leader.'

Realising the game was up, Muhammad Reza, Iran's last Shah, packed his bags and left the country on 16 January. Most Iranians were ecstatic, and when Khomeini boarded an Air France jet to fly into Tehran two weeks later, there was an almost universal feeling that their troubles were now over. On 1 February, Khomeini stepped from his plane, kissed the ground, and proclaimed: 'From now on it is I who will name the government.' Westerners were staggered by Khomeini's welcome, unaware just how widespread his support was in Iran.

For most Iranians, it was a moment of pure joy. The democrats, constitutionalists and liberals had been fighting a common enemy with Khomeini for so long that it never occurred to many of them that he had a very, very different vision of the future from theirs.

CHAPTER 9

Khomeini's Rule

'The day I feel danger to the Islamic Republic, I will cut everybody's hand off. I will do to you what I did to Muhammad Reza.'

Ayatollah Khomeini on opposition to Islamic rule

Khomeini had always been clear that it was his plan to establish an Islamic Republic. Yet few people outside the clergy had taken him at his word. When he went back to his little house in Qom and left the Provisional Revolutionary Government under the control of Mehdi Bazargan, one of the veterans of the National Front, it seemed as if he was content to take a back seat. In fact, he was simply pulling the strings from behind the scenes.

Mullah muscle

It wasn't the Revolutionary Government which held the muscle in the new regime but the Revolutionary Council, a group of Khomeini's most trusted supporters, mostly mullahs. And while Bazargan simply wanted to govern the country, the Revolutionary Council wanted to change it root and branch. On 30 March 1979, a referendum was to be held to decide the future of the state. Bazargan said that the voters should be offered a choice. The Council said that they should be asked only if they accepted or rejected an Islamic Republic. The Council won, and the referendum was carried with an apparently overwhelming majority. Ayatollah Khomeini declared the establishment of the world's first Islamic Republic.

The arms of Islamic control

Gradually, it became clear that the Provisional Government had no more power than the Majlis under the Shah. And new institutions soon appeared to ensure that the Ayatollah's Islamic ideals were being adhered to. First of all, there were the vigilante groups called *komitehs*, which had the power to arbitrarily arrest anyone they thought was un-Islamic. They would burst into homes to pour alcohol away, smash records of Western music and carry the offenders off to jail.

Then there was the green-clad Revolutionary Guard Corps. This was the mullah's private army, recruited through the mosques, and used to crack down on any disruptive elements. And finally there were the revolutionary tribunals. Headed by men like Sadeq Khalkali (notorious for the pleasure he took in strangling cats), these tribunals were designed to summarily 'convict' and execute enemies of Islam – principally members of SAVAK and the former Shah's government.

Together, these organisations set about pummelling Iranians into Islamic line with the same kind of intimidation and zeal that the Pahlavi shahs had used in the modernisation drive. Signs of Western culture quickly disappeared from the streets, women appeared only in the chador, and any signs of dissent were driven underground with brutal efficiency.

The battle over the constitution

Prime Minister Bazargan drew up a new constitution, not so different from that of 1905, but with a president rather than a shah. The master manipulator, Khomeini approved the constitution (after adding provisions barring women from the presidency) and then passed it on to the Assembly of Experts, elected by the mullahs to verify if the constitution agreed with the vision of an Islamic Republic voted for by the Iranian Republic. It did not. Every law voted for by the Majlis could be vetoed by the twelve-man Guardian Council (a group of mullahs appointed largely by Khomeini) if they deemed it contrary to Shari'ah law. And both the Majlis and the Guardian Council had to submit to the wisdom of the faqih, who had special knowledge of the wisdom of God. The faqih had the right to veto all candidates for the Majlis and the presidency. Unsurprisingly, the Assembly of Experts approved Khomeini as the first faqih or Supreme Leader. It was now becoming clear just who was going to be in charge in Iran: Khomeini.

Some members of the Revolutionary Government began to protest, believing Iran was slipping back into a dictatorship. The Revolutionary Guard and Khomeini quickly nipped the dissenters in the bud with a round of snap arrests and fatherly talks.

Asset stripping

The coming of the Revolution gave the Islamic government enormous power over just about every aspect of economic life, and the theological justification to use it. Later on, clerics were to argue that Islamic teaching allows the ownership of private property that someone has earned for themselves, but in the early days of the Republic, the government seized just about everything worth seizing. Within a month of the Revolution, Khomeini had ordered that the possessions of anyone who had got their wealth from contact with the Shah's family should be seized and given to the poor. Seized assets were put under the control of the Bonyad-e Mostazafin – the Foundation of the Disinherited. The banks were nationalised soon after, and then insurance companies. Then, under the Law for the Protection and Expansion of Iranian Industry, the government took over just about every industry in the country, from shipbuilding to local supermarkets.

Finally, the government attempted what Muhammad Reza Shah had tried but failed to achieve – land reform. Some Islamicists argued that all land is God's, and people's ownership of it is 'limited and conditional'. A law passed by the Revolutionary Council in April 1980 tried to confiscate all but the smallest landholdings and redistribute them to the poor. The initial result of this law was chaos, as people disputed confiscated land. Eventually in 1982, the Guardian Council – influenced, perhaps, by the fact that many mullahs were wealthy landowners – began to veto land reform and a number of other laws relating to private property, on the grounds that they violated Islamic teaching. The net result was that a lot of assets seized during the opening years of the Revolution stayed in the hands of those who seized them and were never redistributed to the poor.

The hostage crisis

Then shocking news came through from the USA. Muhammad Reza was in New York. The Americans had let him into the country for medical treatment on a lymphoma. But many Iranians, with the memory of the 1953 coup burning strong, were convinced that the Americans were lining him up for another coup. On 4 November 1979, a large group of students broke into the American embassy in Tehran and took 52 staff hostage.

Bazargan tried to negotiate a deal with the Americans, but Khomeini was quick to praise the hostage-takers, announcing the America was the Great Satan. Bazargan resigned and the Provisional Revolutionary Government resigned with him, leaving the country to be governed by the Revolutionary Council.

The Iran hostage crisis shocked Americans, who had little knowledge of Iran and even less of the 1953 coup. Indeed, it soured Iran–American relations for a long time to come. The whole crisis dragged on for 444 days, during which the Americans made a disastrous failed attempt to rescue the hostages, *Boys' Own* adventure-style. Helicopters were supposed to rendezvous in the Iranian desert outside Tehran with transport planes carrying a commando assault group. Unfortunately, the helicopters hit a sandstorm and crashed into the transport planes, leaving the mission a disaster, the Americans looking very foolish and the Iranians convinced that the US had tried another 1953-style coup.

Neutralising the left

Using this as a pretext, militant Muslim students launched riots attacking any organisation judged as counter-revolutionary, and beat them into bloody submission. Just before this, the elections for the first Majlis had been held, and Khomeini's old friend Abol Bani-Sadr had been made the first president. But Bani-Sadr was no more in control of the country than Bazargan, and Khomeini's drive to Islamicise the country gathered pace, as things like ties were banned, journalists were thrown into prison for un-Islamic comments, and ancient punishments for adultery were revived.

With the liberal opposition on the run, Khomeini finally arranged for the hostages to be set free on 20 January 1981. Khomeini was in charge, and even his friend Bani-Sadr had proved too liberal a president and was soon shuffled off to be replaced by the more compliant Al Rajai. But by that time, Iran was involved in an event much more traumatic than anything either Muhammad Reza or the Islamic Revolution had thrown at them – the Iran–Iraq war.

CHAPTER 10

Iran at War

'[Do] *whatever is necessary and legal* [to prevent Iraq losing the war].'
Ronald Reagan's secret instructions to his administration, 26 November 1983

With Bani-Sadr driven from the Majlis in June 1981, Ayatollah Khomeini may have won the political war. But Bani-Sadr's departure marked the beginning of Iran's bitter civil war. Iran was already fighting a terrible external war with Iraq on its southern border. Now the infant Islamic Republic had an internal war on its hands.

The Mujahedin

The Mujahedin-e Khalq had been a major force in the fight against Muhammad Reza Shah. Formed in 1965, its aim was to create a perfectly equal society that combined Marxism with Islam. It drew support from the poor and middle class, and trained them into an army of guerrillas 100,000 strong. Casualties in the war between SAVAK and the Mujahedin had been high, but it survived until the Revolution. Although regarding clerics as a parasitic class, the Mujahedin tentatively welcomed Khomeini. But when their leader Masoud Rajavi tried to run for president, Khomeini banned him on the grounds that he was 'un-Islamic'.

When Bani-Sadr was ousted, the Mujahedin despaired of getting anything from Khomeini, and began to launch a terror campaign. The first bomb struck just five days after Bani-Sadr's dismissal, killing 74 members of the Islamic Republican Party as they met in Tehran – including Ayatollah Beheshti, Khomeini's second-in-command.

Throughout the summer and autumn of 1981, the Mujahedin planted bomb after bomb, killing more than a thousand mullahs, policemen, Party members – and ordinary people caught in the wrong place. The Revolutionary Guards fought back with even more bloody vengeance. They broke up demonstrations, burst into houses, snatched people from the street and shot anyone with any remote connection to the dissidents. For month after month, 50 people a day went before the firing squads. The Iranians soon learned that the Islamic Republic could be as brutal in its way as the shahs.

As the two opponents slugged it out, the country descended into chaos, while all the time the Iran–Iraq war was going on in the south. Eventually, by early 1982, the terror burned itself out. But now the external war was beginning to take a terrible toll.

'The imposed war'

While the Islamic Revolution was going on, Iran's neighbour to the south, Iraq, had been watching events warily. Iraq's population is 60 per cent Shia, and Saddam Hussein was extremely worried that this Islamic Revolution could be infectious. He also had an eye for the main chance.

Saddam Hussein had just muscled his way to dictatorial control in Iraq, and there was no way he was going to let the Ayatollah ruin it. His Ba'athist party believed that Islam was at the root of many social ills. Rather than risk Iran's Islamic Revolution spreading to Iraq, Saddam must have reasoned, it was surely better to make a pre-emptive strike. Besides, Iraq had all those oil refineries and oil reserves sitting just across the Shatt al-Arab waterway.

At dawn on 22 September 1980, Saddam launched four simultaneous strikes of Iraqi troops across the border into Iran. To urge his troops on, he likened the strike to the Arabs carrying Islam forward in the 7th century and seeing off the fire-worshipping Persians. His armies were well equipped and well trained, and he was convinced that chaotic, revolutionary Iran would quickly yield the territory he craved.

Yet though the Iranians were poorly equipped and trained, they had numbers, and an extraordinary willingness to die in defence of their country – or rather in defence of Islam. Whatever their internal problems, they had just achieved their revolution, and countless Iranians would give their lives to save it.

As soon as Saddam's troops crossed the border in what Iranians came to call 'the imposed war', Khomeini was quick to show Iranians what was at stake. This was not simply a small invasion of one country by another, he pronounced, but a holy war. Saddam's invasion was, in the Ayatollah's words, 'a blasphemy against Islam'. The war against Saddam became a rallying point, uniting the country against a common enemy – and taking some pressure off the regime. Iranian Shia Muslims, brought up since infancy with the story of Hussein martyred at Karbala by the largely Arab Sunnis, couldn't help but see the parallels in this war against Arab invaders. The stakes, Khomeini made clear, were the highest possible.

Human minesweepers

Of all the stories of the Iran–Iraq war, nothing is perhaps quite so shocking as the story of the *Basij*. The Basij (Units of Mobilisation for the Deprived) were designed to give anyone not old enough, or too old, to be a soldier a role in the war. Most Basij-i were young boys and girls. They came from the poorest, most devout families, and volunteered to go to the front in the school holidays. Wearing ragged uniforms, a yellow headband and a brass key round their necks – their key to paradise – their job was to walk through minefields ahead of the soldiers, clearing the way. Thousands of them died this way, confident that they would go to heaven.

The cost of war

The brunt of the first attacks was taken by the Revolutionary Guards, whose commitment to Islam was never in doubt – and young Iranians began to volunteer for them in droves. The Iraqis took the oil port of Khorramshahr and the refinery at Abadan, but they could get no further. The Iranians threw themselves into the defence with such fervour that, although vastly outgunned, they were able to hold up the Iraqis.

Saddam's lightning strike rapidly began to turn into a grinding war of attrition – the first trench warfare since 1918 – and the stakes were so high that neither side would give any quarter. It was a war for survival, for once Khomeini had elevated it to the level of a holy war, it was clear that the Iranians couldn't stop until they had achieved complete victory over the Iraqis. It had to go on until the bitter end – or until Khomeini changed his mind. 'War, war until victory' became the Iranian slogan. In fact, the war went on for eight terrible years, and the cost to both countries was appalling.

Over three-quarters of a million Iranians lost their lives in this ghastly episode – more than the entire American losses in the Second World War, and out of a population less than a quarter of the size. But even the sheer casualty numbers fail to convey just how terrible it all was for the soldiers involved. This wasn't a 'clean' war, but a horrible, dirty, grim fight to the death in which each side tried to inflict maximum damage on the other. Countless Iranians who survived the war came home traumatised and disfigured, with bits of their body missing, or their minds shattered through the sheer horror of it all. The combatants on both sides were exposed to chemical warfare on a scale beyond anything seen before or since.

The American playing field

Such were the human resources of Iran that it might well have finally won the war if it hadn't been for the intervention of the Americans on the side of Saddam Hussein. The Americans provided the Iraqis with satellite and AWACs pictures revealing Iranian positions. They supplied the Iraqis with arms, and with money and food that kept the Iraqi economy afloat. They conducted a series of diplomatic moves to isolate Iran. In December 1983, for instance, the US took Iraq off the 'terrorist list' and added Iran, then started 'Operation Staunch' to prevent anyone supplying Iran with arms. Perhaps most importantly, they conducted the 'tanker war' in the Persian Gulf. Ostensibly this was meant to protect tankers taking oil from Kuwait, but it effectively destroyed Iran's navy.

The extraordinary thing is that all this help came after Saddam had embarked on a programme to build nuclear weapons, and when he was known to have used banned chemical and biological weapons. Indeed, the US apparently supplied him with some of the bacteria and fungus cultures needed to make biological weapons. There's no doubt that the Beirut bombs and the hostage crisis in Lebanon (see Chapter 11) had given Iran a bad image in American eyes – but the hostage crisis was over long before American support for Iraq really kicked in. The real reason is that it looked as if Iraq might lose. If Iran won, the whole oil-producing region might be destabilised. The ideal result for the Americans was a stalemate – and their idea was simply to provide a 'level playing field' in which Iran's sheer numbers were balanced by Iraqi arms and US backing.

The course of the war

The Iran–Iraq war took place in four phases. In the first phase, which lasted from 1980 to 1981, the Iranians resisted the Iraqi offensive, halting their advance just beyond Khorramshahr with their patchwork force of Revolutionary Guards, police and officers of the Shah released from jail.

In the second phase, from 1982 to 1984, the professional Iranian army finally joined the patchwork force at the front for a ferocious assault on the Iraqis. All the territory the Iraqis had captured was regained. Then the Iraqis began to use mustard gas and the Iranian advance ground to a halt. A deadly stalemate left the front almost exactly where it had been four years earlier.

The third phase saw the combatants entrenching themselves doggedly for a further two years. The fourth phase from 1986 to 1987 saw both sides going all out to end the war. While the Iraqis sent missile after missile at Iranian cities, firing Soviet Scuds nightly at Tehran, the Iranians drove bloodily into Iraq in offensives called, ironically, Karbala 4 and Karbala 5. The cost of these offensives in human lives was appalling. Over half the 100,000 Basij-i died as they walked through minefields left by the Iraqis, along with a quarter of the Revolutionary Guard officers. Through all this terrible slaughter, Khomeini and Saddam carried on, certain that neither could stop until they had beaten their opponents utterly.

Finally, though, on 18 July 1988, even Khomeini was persuaded – after eight ghastly years – that Iran couldn't take any more, and he agreed to the ceasefire suggested by the UN.

CHAPTER 11

Spreading the Islamic Revolution?

*'We will export our experiences to the world.
This export will certainly result in the bloom-
ing of the buds of victory and independence
and in the implementation of Islamic teach-
ings among enslaved nations.'*
Ayatollah Khomeini in 1987, after the death
of 402 Iranians at the *haj* in Mecca

Many Iranians fought for the 1979 revolution
because they hoped it would free their
country, or because they hoped it would make
Iran a truly Islamic country. Ayatollah Khomeini
always had something bigger in mind. Iran was
just the start. He and many of his fellow clerics
wanted to create a new Islamic world order. The

idea of nations, Khomeini argued, is a Western notion devised to divide Islam. His vision was to unite all Islamic peoples – and the drive to unity would come from Iran. Significantly, he talked not of Iran, but the nation of Islam.

Many clerics disagreed with Khomeini's desire to export the Islamic Revolution, but Khomeini's influence was paramount as Supreme Leader. Moreover, the assault on Iran from Iraq with American support made Iranians feel very vulnerable, and even those who weren't completely in tune with the idea of spreading the Revolution could see that it might be good to have a buffer of like-minded states around Iran.

Export duty

There's no doubt that the coming of the Islamic Revolution, and Khomeini's stirring words, created a buzz among Shia people well beyond Iran's borders. Hundreds of excited young Shias from all over the Arab world went to Iran to the military training camps run by the Revolutionary Guard. There they learned how to handle guns, how to plant explosives and how to fire rocket launchers, at the same time as learning the meaning of the Islamic Revolution.

Arab leaders, especially those of the Gulf

states, grew understandably nervous. Like Iraq, many of these states, such as Bahrain and Kuwait, had substantial Shia populations – and most of them were ruled by pro-Western Sunni oligarchs who, in Khomeini's picture of the world, seemed the same kind of oppressor as the Shah.

Soon, it turned out they were right to be nervous. In December 1981, a group of young products of the Iranian camps were picked up boarding a plane in Dubai for Bahrain. Interrogation revealed a plot to bring down the Sheikh of Bahrain. Dhow-loads of guns and grenades were soon discovered, along with communications equipment smuggled into Bahrain via the Iranian embassy. In December 1983, a string of bombs exploded in Kuwait. Although none of the bombers were Iranian, it was felt that Iran was behind them, and the Iranians didn't deny it.

At the same time, Khomeini was trying to turn the *haj*, the annual Islamic pilgrimage to Mecca, into a rally for the Revolution. In 1982 and 1983 the haj was disrupted by 100,000 Iranians carrying placards and shouting slogans. For a few years, the Arab authorities banned Iranians from the haj, but in 1987, 155,000 Iranians arrived with instructions from Khomeini to disrupt the ceremonies with demonstrations. As they surged through the streets, they met with Arab riot police. In the ensuing crush, 402 people died.

Despite the tension created by such events, Khomeini's ideas actually found few converts outside Iran. It may be that the Shias of Iraq and the Gulf states, though united with Iran by religion, were divided by race and language. They are Arab people, speaking Arabic languages, not Iranian.

Lebanon and Hezbollah

One place where Shias did listen to Tehran was Lebanon. In the early 1980s, Lebanon provided the base from which the Palestine Liberation Organisation (PLO) was launching its attacks on Israel. In April 1982, Israel, exasperated by these attacks, sent its armies into Lebanon to pound the city of Beirut where the PLO were holed up. The Arab world was incensed by the Israeli invasion, and passions in Lebanon were raised to boiling point. Two months later, a troop of Iranian Revolutionary Guards moved into Lebanon's Baaka valley, and turned the town of Baalbek into 'little Tehran'. Amid the turmoil of events, their presence was barely noticed, but it was a sign of Iran's eagerness to export their revolution.

More significantly, though, the Iranians were

providing funds and technical support for Hezbollah – a collection of groups based at Lebanese mosques and dedicated to fighting the cause of Islam. The significance was that Hezbollah was behind the first major terrorist attacks now linked with what is called 'Islamic terrorism'.

With the Israeli army pounding Beirut with its guns and bombs, the United States formed a Multi-National Force (MNF) with a handful of other Western nations. In August 1982, the MNF went into Beirut and extracted Yasser Arafat and the PLO heads successfully, but as tensions in Lebanon began to increase, the MNF went in again to act as peacekeepers. Now, for Iran, America was confirming its identity as the Great Satan, bent on interfering with Islamic affairs.

On 18 April 1983, a van exploded outside the American embassy in Beirut, killing 58 Americans and Lebanese. Six months later, another blast killed 241 US Marines in their Beirut barracks. Then 47 French soldiers in the MNF were killed by another bomb. All these bombs were linked to the Baaka valley and Hezbollah.

The US was badly shaken, and within a few months the MNF had left Beirut altogether. Even as they pulled out, Islamic terrorists, deprived of large targets, were trying another tactic. In February 1984 Frank Regier, the first Western hostage, was kidnapped. Others followed, and images of hooded hostages with guns pointed to their heads horrified the Western world.

Iran falters

Yet the mood was already changing in Iran. Far from bringing Iran new friends, the exporting of the Islamic Revolution was driving the country into isolation, as Western nations combined to condemn Iran as a sponsor of terrorism. As exports and imports both began to dry up, the economy was collapsing. Unemployment was rife. And there were devastating shortages of even basic foodstuffs. What little was available was being sold only at astronomical black market prices far beyond the poor.

Meanwhile, the physical effects of the war with Iraq were becoming severe. Thousands of young Iranians were dying every day. Thousands were coming home maimed and battered. And yet there was no sign of any progress – or any end. Moreover, the Americans and other Western nations were throwing all their military technology on the side of the Iraqis, while the Iranians were relying at best on the hardware supplied by the Americans in the Shah's time but now breaking down, with no spare parts to repair it.

At the same time, various mullahs were beginning to question the theological justification of both the war and exporting Islam. Islam does not condone attacks on other Muslims. Nor can anyone, according to Iranian Shi'ism, declare *jihad* or holy war but the Hidden Imam on his return.

In spring 1985, demonstrations against the war and the government broke out across Iran. The government responded by branding the protesters as left-wing agitators, and sent in Revolutionary Guards and vigilantes to pick up anyone thought to be a ringleader. But clearly something had to give. Moreover, even the most hardline among the clerics began to realise that they might lose the war with Iraq – and so the Revolution – if they didn't try to get a little help from outside soon.

It was against this background that Iran's stance on terrorism began to shift. First, in June 1985, when Lebanese Shia hijacked TWA flight 847 between Athens and Rome, Ali Rafsanjani, the speaker of the Iranian Majlis, disclaimed any Iranian responsibility. It was the first time Iran had attempted to distance itself from its

Lebanese partners. The Ayatollah did nothing to silence Rafsanjani. Something had clearly changed. Moreover, Rafsanjani began to pull strings behind the scenes to get the hijacked passengers of the TWA flight released. Indeed, President Ronald Reagan publicly thanked Rafsanjani for his help.

The Iran–Contra affair

Now began one of the strangest events of the tussle between America and Iran – the Iran–Contra affair. In May 1985, a Boeing 707, painted black, landed at Tehran in an atmosphere of great secrecy. On board were two Americans on a clandestine mission, John Poindexter and Oliver North – both part of America's National Security Council. Besides the normal diplomatic gifts, they had with them the vital spare parts for the Iranians' American anti-tank missiles.

As it later transpired, their mission, authorised secretly by President Reagan, was to supply Iran with arms in exchange for Iranian help in freeing American kidnap victims held hostage in the Lebanon. This directly contradicted the USA's stated policy of never negotiating with terrorists or with countries like Iran that support them. When news of the deal leaked out in November 1986, it was all hugely embarrassing for the

Reagan government. Even more damaging, it turned out that North had diverted the $48 million profits from the deal to fund the Contras. The Contras were the revolutionary group in Nicaragua trying to bring down the socialist Sandinista government – and Congress had specifically voted against funding them. After a long and highly publicised hearing, both Poindexter and North, clearly scapegoats, were convicted of charges of obstructing justice, then released on appeal.

The end of the war

Meanwhile in Iran, Rafsanjani was heavily criticised by many for dealing with the Great Satan. Yet Khomeini's voice was not among the critics, and Rafsanjani survived. Indeed, he was put in control of Karbala 4 and Karbala 5, Iran's great thrusts into Iraqi territory using the American arms. These took the Iranians close to Basra but no further. And so the war dragged on with no sign of victory for one side or another.

Increased Western support for the Iraqis was beginning to tell. The Iranian economy was in tatters. Food shortages were all too common, inflation was rampant and unemployment hit over 40 per cent. And almost half a million young Iranians had come home in coffins – or been buried where they died. Even so, the war hadn't yet come to the Iranian heartland. Then in February 1988, Scud missiles began raining down on Tehran. Millions of people fled from the city.

The Satanic Verses

With the end of the Iran–Iraq war, Iran seemed to be opening up to the world again. Rafsanjani was talking to the European powers, and strengthening relations with West Germany in particular. However, it was all too much for Ayatollah Khomeini, now almost 90. In September 1988, the day the war ended, a book called *The Satanic Verses* was published in Britain. In a wide-ranging fable, the author Salman Rushdie depicts Mohammad as Mahound, a word for the devil, and gives prostitutes the names of his wives. The original Satanic Verses are parts of the Koran which a 10th-century historian, al-Tabari, said were omitted on the grounds that Gabriel claimed they came from the devil. Ayatollah Khomeini was so offended that on 14 February 1988 he issued a fatwa sentencing Rushdie to death, and calling on Muslims to execute anyone connected with the book's publication. As Rushdie went into hiding, and bookshops quickly cleared their shelves, Rafsanjani's efforts at establishing links with the West were torpedoed. Rafsanjani suggested that the fatwa was simply religious and nothing to do with relationships between states. President Ali Khamenei suggested that a pardon might be available if Rushdie apologised. But it was too late; Khomeini's words had done their damage.

The situation was becoming desperate. Finally, in July 1988, Rafsanjani called together all the major figures in the government. They agreed that the only way to save the Revolution was to save Iran – and that meant calling a halt to the war. But it needed Khomeini to endorse the decision. On 18 July, reluctantly, he did, announcing:

'I had promised to fight to the last drop of my blood and to my last breath. Taking this decision was more deadly than drinking hemlock.'

At once, Iran and Iraq called a ceasefire and began to enter into negotiations. Iran's drive to export the Islamic Revolution had ground to halt, at least for while, and in less than a year the driver himself, Ayatollah Khomeini, was dead.

CHAPTER 12

After Khomeini

'We love all the people in the world, and we want them to love us in return. Resentments should be turned to love and kindness.'
Iranian president Muhammad Khatami,
quoted in the *New York Times*,
1 February 1998

When Ayatollah Khomeini died, there was a national outpouring of grief. Even those who were opposed to him acknowledged that he had been a giant. Millions lined the streets of Tehran for his funeral, and his tomb in southern Iran is now a vast shrine, visited by thousands of people every month.

The mullahs were quick to find a successor to Khomeini. Their choice was the then president, Ali Khamenei. It was a choice clearly guided by politics rather than religion, since Ali Khamenei, though a hojjat ol-eslam, was not an ayatollah, and in order to make him Supreme Leader the clerics rapidly had to confer the title of ayatollah on him – much against the time-honoured tradition of slowly acquiring the title. Khamenei was deemed a safe pair of hands.

Rafsanjani rises

As Khamenei became Supreme Leader, his place as president was taken by Ali Rafsanjani, the man who had negotiated with the USA on the arms-for-hostages deal. And it was Rafsanjani who was to be the visible leader of the country for the next eight years, rather than Khamenei.

Rafsanjani was a cleric – a hojjat ol-eslam like Khamenei. He was also a hero of the clerical opposition to the Shah and of the 1979 revolution. But he wasn't a hardliner; he was a pragmatist who believed that it was necessary to get the economy working and to engage with the West, even the Great Satan America, where necessary.

Hardliners vs. pragmatists

In the years following Khomeini's death, Iranian politics has been a constant struggle between the hardliners and the pragmatists. Like the hardliners, the pragmatists are still largely religious men – there's little chance for those who don't have the ear of the clerics to make their way in politics – but the pragmatists are willing to adjust their policies to fit realities. The ultra-conservative and ultra-radical believe that such compromises are fatal to the Revolution. Sometimes the door has opened and the pragmatists and reformists have made headway. Just as often, however, the hardliners have slammed the door shut again.

With the ascendancy of Rafsanjani, the pragmatists were setting the agenda for a while. First to go was the idea of exporting the Revolution. In 1990, the Shias in southern Iraq staged an uprising, expecting support from both Iran and the West. None came. Saddam Hussein repressed the Shia rebellion brutally, yet Iran said nothing. An unnamed Iranian diplomat told the *New York Times* at the time: 'The revolution ... died when Iraq bombed old shrines in Najaf and Karbala, without an Iranian response ... it died when the country decided to stop exporting its Islamic revolution and concentrate on the mess inside.'

That is exactly what Rafsanjani tried to do, but his attempts to bring the economy under control hit the poorest hardest. Removing the subsidies on chicken, electricity and gas, and telephones,

Corruption Tehran style

Although the Islamic Revolution was supposed to sweep away the corruption of the Shah's time, the Islamic Republic has developed its own fair share of corruption, as is so often the case where power lies in the hands of a few. When the Islamic state took things over in the name of the Revolution, it wasn't always redistributed in a socially equable way. Many of Tehran's best homes, taken from rich royalists, are now the homes of prominent mullahs and their friends. Every politician is believed to have fingers in lots of lucrative pies. The *bonyads*, the foundations set up to deal with seized assets, are a byword for corruption, lining the pockets of those in the loop. And for those with a little cash, all kinds of strict Islamic rules can be bent.

improving tax collection, clearing the shanties and so on, all took their toll on those at the bottom of the financial ladder. The poor responded with riots; and it was the hardliners who sent in the Revolutionary Guards to put them down. And so the balance between hardliners and pragmatists kept on shifting.

Towards the end of Rafsanjani's presidency, things seemed to be shifting back in favour of the hardliners – especially in the wake of the USA's decision in 1995 to slap a trade embargo on Iran as a sponsor of state terrorism. And then in the 1997 elections for the presidency, something remarkable happened.

Muhammad Khatami

The conservative candidate for president was Ali Nateq-Noori, a solid, reliable hardliner. With all the power of the cleric-controlled media behind him, and the mullahs pushing his candidacy in the mosques, it seemed a foregone conclusion that he would win. Yet to keep the left happy, Ayatollah Khamenei had allowed one moderate candidate, Muhammad Khatami, to stand. He was a cleric, so even if the unthinkable happened, it wouldn't be a disaster. Then the unthinkable did happen.

As the elections neared, Khatami's mild, almost childlike manner began to strike a chord with Iranians, especially women. As he toured the country speaking humbly and enthusiastically about rights, freedom and the rule of law, countless Iranians flocked to hear him – and began to believe that his message of gentle reform and openness might hold the hope of a better future. 'The government doesn't give the people the opportunity to grow', Khatami said, and many believed that it was time Iranians were given that chance.

Tehran spring

When the elections came, it was as if, after long years of bitter disappointment, Iranians had rediscovered hope. The turnout was almost double the previous election, and Khatami was voted home with an overwhelming 70 per cent of the vote. Among women and young people, support for Khatami was almost universal. As the handsome, urbane new president appeared on television, quietly announcing his plan of reform, people began to talk of him not just as Iran's J. F. Kennedy but as Iran's Gorbachev. Khatami's desire to emphasise the gentler side of Islam seemed full of promise. At his rallies, he asked people to stop chanting the Revolution's mantra, 'Death to ...' (whoever was deemed the enemy). 'I stand for life', he said, 'not death. Ours is the God of love.'

Muhammad Khatami: Ayatollah Gorbachev

Muhammad Khatami was a liberal theologian in the best Islamic tradition. Schooled in Shia Islam, Persian history and Greek philosophy at Qom in the early 1960s, he was also fluent in English and German as well as Farsi and Arabic. He lived in Germany for two years, and developed a real understanding of Western values. After the Islamic Revolution he became culture minister, a post he held for a decade until the conservatives drove him from office in 1992 for his too liberal views – once allowing a woman to perform a solo show in Tehran, against the hardline taboo. Exiled from politics for five years, he became convinced that blocking out Western culture would merely give it allure as forbidden fruit. When he came to power in 1997, he was convinced that he could find Iran's future through gradual change.

In 2000, reformers won a big majority in the Majlis elections, and in 2001 Khatami was re-elected with an even larger 78 per cent of the vote. As Iran opened up to dialogue with the West, and the severest strictures of the Islamic regime were loosened, outsiders began to talk of 'a Tehran spring' and many of the talented liberals who had left Iran in the hardest years of the Revolution began to return.

Conservative fightback

Yet the hardliners were far from beaten. Reformers may have had the upper hand in the Majlis, but everything they do is vetted by the Guardian Council. Of the 295 reforms introduced by the Majlis between 2000 and 2004, 111 were vetoed entirely by the Guardian Council. Many of the rest were severely watered down. And so the hoped-for reforms never seemed to come. Moreover, the conservative backlash began to take a more active form. Reformist intellectuals were murdered or imprisoned. Students were imprisoned and beaten. Newspapers pushing the reform agenda were closed down.

By 2004, Iranians were beginning to lose faith in the reformers, who clearly couldn't deliver what they promised. Khatami lost his aura as the man who could change things. It seemed that he was too weak to make any of his reforms stick, and many of his strongest supporters were turning against him. Worse still, the unreformed economy still left Iran's vast underclass in as dire straits as ever. The gradually growing prosperity of the better off served only to underline this.

When the 2004 Majlis elections came round, the Guardian Council banned over 2,000 reform- ist candidates from standing – including 82 who had been deputies in the previous Majlis. Dis- appointed again, many Iranians refused to vote. As a result, the conservatives swept back into power and Khatami was left as a lame-duck presi- dent for his final year in office. Then in 2005, with Khatami gone, the hardliners' resurgence seemed complete with the election of the ultra- conservative Mahmoud Ahmadinejad.

CHAPTER 13

The Blacksmith's Son

'Iran is a learned nation. It is a civilised nation. It is a history-making nation ... You know and we know: you need us far more than we need you.'

Iranian President Mahmoud Ahmadinejad, 2006

In June 2005, Ali Rafsanjani stood for election as Iran's president. As one of the heroes of the Islamic Revolution, twice president and a statesman of world standing, he seemed the clear favourite to outsiders. Yet he was beaten utterly by Mahmoud Ahmadinejad, a blacksmith's son, little known to people outside Iran. Just as the reform-minded Khatami had come from nowhere to take 70 per cent of the vote in Iran's 1997 presidential election, so Ahmadinejad did in 2005.

But there was a world of difference between Khatami and Ahmadinejad. Khatami was urbane, conciliatory, reform-minded. Ahmadinejad is raw, confrontational and ultra-conservative.

Ahmadinejad, of course, had the backing of the hardliners in Iran's power structure. For too many of the more conservative mullahs, Khatami represented a dangerous shift to secularisation in Iran, a creeping Westernisation which threatens Islamic values. Rafsanjani was of the same mould. So the hardline mullahs put all their considerable resources into making life difficult for the reformers and using the power of the pulpit to drive home Ahmadinejad's candidacy. Yet Ahmadinejad has his own strong appeal too – beyond the heavy hand of the hardline mullahs.

The 'people's friend'

Many Iranians voted for Ahmadinejad because he seemed to offer something that Rafsanjani did not. With their openness to Western values, the reformers have become tainted by them – and seem, to some, inextricably linked with the well-to-do living in their smart apartments in the north of Tehran, while the less well-off are packed into the shanties and squalid blocks of the south.

Honest, hard-working, devout and from a

poor background – unlike most other politicians, it was said – Ahmadinejad had an obvious appeal to the mass of Iran's underprivileged. His simple message of a return to austerity, honesty, 'family values' and pride in religion and the nation found powerful echoes with the traditionally-minded working class. Ahmadinejad refused to spend a penny on his election campaign, but with the mullahs speaking on his behalf in mosques across the land, this became a strength, not a weakness.

Who is Mahmoud Ahmadinejad?

Born in Garmsar near Tehran in 1956, Mahmoud Ahmadinejad is one of a blacksmith's seven children. As a teenager, he came 130th in the nationwide exams and won a place at the prestigious University of Science and Technology in Tehran, where he studied engineering. This was in the 1970s, when Iran's universities were rife with political activism against the Shah that saw left-wing secular extremists clash with religious radicals. The young Ahmadinejad joined the radicals. By the time he gained his PhD he was a well-known hardliner, and he took due part in the 1979 revolution. Some Americans claim that he was one of the ringleaders in the seizure of hostages at the American embassy. He insists he wasn't there, and several of his opponents concur. In the 1980s, Ahmadinejad fought in the Iran–Iraq war, then joined the Revolutionary Guard. Apparently, he became head of a squad whose purpose was to assassinate 'enemies of the Revolution' – a task in which he was said to be brutal and efficient. It's possible he may have travelled to Vienna to kill a Kurdish dissident.

After the war, Ahmadinejad was a rising political star, becoming governor of Ardabil province in 1994. But when the reform-minded Khatami became president, his career stalled and he went back to university as a lecturer, where he ran a radical fundamentalist militia called the Ansar-e Hizbollah (Brotherhood of the Party of God).

THE BLACKSMITH'S SON • 167

Yet Ahmadinejad's zeal and his working-class credentials found favour with the conservatives among the clerics, who clearly felt that by appealing to the underclasses they could win back some of the ground lost to the reformers. With their backing, Ahmadinejad became mayor of Tehran in 2003 – elected with a turnout of just 12 per cent.

By the time the 2005 presidential elections came round, Ahmadinejad was already well known in Tehran for his simple lifestyle and his hardline views.

Ahmadinejad abroad

Although there were accusations of fraud about the election and the turnout was low, Ahmadinejad undoubtedly does tap into a vein of genuine feeling. It might be a mistake to assume, as some Western politicians have, that he has simply been levered into power by a coterie of hardline mullahs – and that they can somehow diminish his influence by appealing over his head to the

Iranian people. Indeed, such an approach might just increase support for him.

There's no doubt that Ahmadinejad's election sent shockwaves through the Western world. With Khatami in power, Western governments had felt that there was at least someone who was open to negotiation and reason if the right approach was found. Ahmadinejad seemed from a different planet.

The West was considerably taken aback when Ahmadinejad unapologetically announced shortly after his election that he was determined to go ahead with Iran's nuclear programme (see Chapter 14). Yet European politicians hoped that they could at least talk about it with him in the normal diplomatic manner. They were in for a rude awakening.

In an article in *The Observer* (15 January 2006), Jason Burke describes a meeting at the UN building in New York in September 2005 between Ahmadinejad and the Foreign Ministers of Britain, France and Germany. The ministers were clearly expecting some kind of rapprochement. Instead, Ahmadinejad left them aghast, saying: 'Do not dare to threaten us with sanctions or you will regret it. You do just what your American masters tell you to do.' The ministers were left almost tongue-tied with shock at this blunt, undiplomatic tone. Burke reports how one unnamed official said afterwards: 'No one could believe what had just happened. All the rules that we had been playing to – and have been playing to for years – had been overturned. He was just not speaking our language. It was as if he had just walked in from the boondocks covered in dust.'

If Ahmadinejad's approach to the nuclear issue was shocking to the West, his comments about Israel and the Jews seemed even more inflammatory. His declaration to a rally in Tehran in October 2005 that 'Israel should be wiped off the map' met with universal condemnation in the West, and it was followed up by his denial of the Holocaust as a myth. Following the imprisonment of the British historian David Irving in Austria for Holocaust denial, Ahmadinejad announced in January 2006 that Tehran would hold a 'scientific' conference to question the authenticity of the Holocaust. Ever since the 1979 revolution, Iran has taken the line that Israel's denial of the Palestinians' territory is an affront to Islam, but Ahmadinejad seems to be taking it to extremes.

Ahmadinejad's Iran

Some commentators have wondered whether Ahmadinejad is simply blustering to frighten off the West, but his behaviour in Iran suggests that he's completely sincere. Since Ahmadinejad came to power, much of the tolerance that came in the Khatami era has been rolled back.

On the lighter side, Western-style burger bars have closed down, young couples are no longer

The Mohammad cartoon

When a Danish newspaper published a cartoon linking Mohammad to terrorism, there was outrage across the Muslim world, with widespread protests and attacks on Danish embassies. Taking up Ahmadinejad's claims that the Holocaust is a myth, Iran's biggest-selling newspaper, *Haramshi*, decided to run a competition to find a cartoon satirising the Holocaust in retaliation – to show the West just what 'freedom of the press' means.

seen holding hands in public, and few girls wear make-up. On a more serious note, left-wing newspapers have begun to disappear and dissidents have found themselves arrested. Ahmadinejad's determination to crack down on Iran's universities seems typical. The universities are seen as hotbeds of pro-democracy movements. So student activists have been jailed, undesirable lecturers have been sacked and there are moves to subject every member of staff to a stringent religious test. Recently, an aide of Ahmadinejad has been overseeing the burial of the bodies of martyrs, such as soldiers who died in the Iran–Iraq war, inside university campuses. Student activists are certain that the aim behind this bizarre move is to open the universities to armed militias.

Preparing for the Hidden Imam

Meanwhile, Ahmadinejad has been stirring up Shia religious fervour by leading a campaign to prepare people for the return of the Hidden Imam. Over half a million people make a pilgrimage to the Jamkaran shrine near Qom every week to pray for his return. Ahmadinejad has allocated huge sums to renovate the shrine, and there are talks of building a railway from Tehran to Jamkaran. Some mullahs believe Ahmadinejad's

Pictures on the wall

Giant murals have adorned Tehran's walls and billboards since the early days of the Islamic Revolution. The first murals, all painted carefully by hand, were of Ayatollah Khomeini and other religious leaders, or of heroism in the Iran–Iraq war. One powerful image shows the martyrdom of thirteen-year-old Hossein Fadimeh, who strapped on a bomb belt to crawl beneath an Iraqi tank and blow himself up. Nowadays, most new murals are printed rather than painted by hand, and under Ahmadinejad have taken a strongly anti-Zionist line. One of the most striking shows the Palestinian female suicide bomber Reem Saleh al-Riyashi, with her baby in one arm and a gun in the other.

decision to make a political issue of the return is a ploy to manipulate the religiously inclined. The leading cleric Ayatollah Montazeri says: 'Using the 12th Imam for political purposes and telling people to prepare the streets to await his return is wrong and a misuse of Islam. Nobody knows when he is going to return.'

Some commentators in Iran fear that Ahmadinejad's emphasis on the Hidden Imam is a step on the path to sweeping away the democratic element in Iran's government and turning it into a theocratic dictatorship. Ahmadinejad's mentor Ayatollah Mesbah-Yazdi questions the need for elections. He argues that the government's Islamic element should always override its republican element and officials should get their authority from God, not from people's votes. Ahmadinejad's supporters claim that, in talking about the return of the Hidden Imam, he is merely emphasising the purist values of the Revolution. It remains to be seen who is right.

CHAPTER 14

Nuclear Iran

> '*It will be impossible to get* [the Iranians] *to give up* [on their nuclear programme], *to come down to zero.*'
>
> Unnamed European diplomat quoted in the *Guardian*, 24 March 2006

Ironically, it was the US – now the harshest opponents of Iran's nuclear development – who first encouraged Iran down the nuclear path back in the 1950s. Perhaps to recover some of the cost of the oil that America was buying from Iran, the US urged the Shah to invest in nuclear power facilities, which might be provided by American companies. The Shah agreed, famously saying: 'Petroleum is a noble material, much too valuable to burn.'

The Shah's nuclear power

In 1967, Iran began to run its first, US-supplied, reactor at the Tehran Nuclear Research Centre (TNRC). The following year, Iran joined the Nuclear Non-proliferation Treaty (NPT), and embarked on a programme to create 23 power stations across the country by 2000 with US help.

Construction of Iran's first nuclear power station at Bushehr, to provide electricity for Shiraz, was well under way by the time the Islamic Revolution came in 1979, and the German firm Kraftwerk-Union AG was making the reactors in conjunction with US contractors. For a variety of reasons, work on the Bushehr plant came to a halt after the Revolution. Then, in the Iran–Iraq war, the site was badly bombed.

After the war, President Rafsanjani approached Kraftwerk to supply the rest of the equipment for Bushehr. Now, however, the US was dead set against nuclear power in Iran, and leaned on Kraftwerk to refuse. US pressure made sure no one else in the West would supply Iran either, so in 1990 Iran completed a deal with Russia to supply the reactors for Bushehr, and in 1991 made a deal with China to supply converters to make uranium hexafluoride – the precursor for uranium fuel. Throughout the 1990s, wrangling went on between Iran and Russia over issues like what to do with nuclear waste, while the US kept applying pressure to Russia to back out, arguing that the Bushehr plant would help train a generation of Iranian scientists in the skill needed to make a nuclear bomb.

Why Iran wants nuclear power

Many critics of Iran believe that its real interest in nuclear power is in developing nuclear weapons. Iran is so rich in oil and natural gas, they say, that it can have no possible need of nuclear energy. However, many Iranians see it differently. Iran has huge uranium ore resources – with, it's said, well over a third of the energy capacity of its oil reserves. With a large and growing population, the country has its own substantial energy needs. Nearly all this energy comes from oil, but, vast though the oil reserves are, the Iranians argue, there will come a time when they will run out – and if Iran is using so much for its own energy needs, then they will run out that much quicker. Following the Shah, they argue that oil is too precious a commodity – the raw material for a host of products such as plastics – to simply burn up to make electricity. Moreover, so much oil is burned in Iran that it has very quickly become one of the world's most polluted countries. So there's a legitimate case for Iran developing alternative energy sources, including nuclear energy. Moreover, the Iranians argue, since Iran signed the NPT, the number of nuclear power stations around the world has mushroomed – there are now over 1,100. Why shouldn't Iran have them?

Iran's hidden fuel-maker

Despite the US opposition, it seemed as if Iran's programme was entirely in accordance with its obligations under the NPT – which basically mean keeping the International Atomic Energy Agency (IAEA) informed, and allowing inspections to ensure that nuclear facilities are entirely for peaceful purposes. Then, in 2003, the West discovered that Iran had two previously unknown nuclear facilities – an underground plant at Natanz for enriching uranium and a heavy water plant at Arak – and that these had been in development since the mid-1980s.

Making nuclear fuel

Typically, uranium ore is turned into uranium fuel for nuclear reactors in several stages. First it's crushed, ground and purified into a powder called yellowcake. Then it's heated to convert it into the gas uranium hexafluoride (conversion). Finally, the gas is spun in a centrifuge to separate out the heavier uranium isotopes needed for the reaction (enrichment).

With only a single nuclear power plant, critics of Iran believed, there was no need for it to have its own nuclear enrichment facilities. Development of enrichment facilities implied a wish to develop nuclear weapons. Iran's secrecy about Natanz only fuelled suspicions.

Caught red-handed, President Khatami went on Iranian TV on 20 February 2003 to tell the nation about Natanz and Arak and various other nuclear facilities, and invited the IAEA to come and inspect them. Iran argued that it was not required to declare the existence of enrichment facilities, unless it was actually making fuel. The IAEA countered that there was an issue of trust at stake. When IAEA inspectors visited Natanz in summer 2003 and discovered traces of enriched uranium, their worst fears seemed confirmed. Iranian nuclear scientists suggested, with some grounds, that these traces were merely contamination. But the IAEA sealed up the Natanz plant and issued Iran with an ultimatum to reveal the full details of its nuclear activities.

Throughout 2004 and 2005, negotiations carried on between the IAEA and Iran, with the lead being taken by the EU3 – France, Britain and Germany. With Khatami as president, the EU3 felt that progress was being made. In the summer of 2005, Ayatollah Khamenei even issued a fatwa against the development of nuclear weapons. At first, it seemed as if Ahmadinejad would go down the same path.

Iran's nuclear facilities

Besides the Bushehr nuclear power station on the Gulf Coast, due to open late in 2006, Iran has a range of other nuclear facilities. At Saghand in central Iran, there are three mines with combined reserves of about 800 million tonnes of uranium. Nearby is the Ardkan milling complex, capable of making 60–70 tonnes of yellowcake a year. Guhane is another mine complex in the south with a facility for making 24 tonnes of yellowcake a year. Isfahan is a nuclear reprocessing facility. Arak is a heavy water production plant. Natanz is an underground complex of gas centrifuges designed to produce enriched uranium by spinning uranium hexafluoride gas. This is the site that all the fuss is about. It currently has about 200 centrifuges up and running, but the plan is for 5,000.

Iran's nuclear offensive

Then, in autumn 2005, the new Iranian president began to adopt a more strident tone, and negotiations immediately ran into difficulties. To the outrage of the West, Ahmadinejad announced that Iran would carry on its nuclear programme whatever the IAEA said. As the diplomatic battle became increasingly heated, the USA and Iran were drawn into exchanging veiled and not-so-veiled threats. Defense Secretary Donald Rumsfeld refused to rule out air strikes against Iran's nuclear facilities, while Iran replied that if anyone attacks, 'we will give the enemy a lesson that will be remembered throughout history!' Meanwhile, back home, Ahmadinejad was stirring up rallies in Tehran by getting people to chant: 'Nuclear power is our inalienable right!'

In January 2006, as talks seemed deadlocked, Iranian nuclear scientists broke the IAEA's seals on their nuclear power facilities. The IAEA insisted that it had a 'lack of confidence' in Iran's intentions, and urged Iran to halt all research and cooperate with inspectors. In Vienna, members of the IAEA committee led by Muhammad El Baradei debated furiously over whether to report Iran to the UN Security Council. Russia,

American consistency

One of Iran's arguments with the USA is that its nuclear policy is not consistent. While Iran and other countries belong to the NPT, and are willing to open their nuclear facilities to inspection, many of America's friends – such as Israel, Iran's *bête noire* – have stayed outside the NPT and developed not just nuclear power but nuclear weapons without any criticism from the USA. And it was unfortunate that just as Iran's talks with the EU3 were reaching crisis point in Vienna in early March 2006, George Bush was in India giving their nuclear programme the green light even though they remained outside the NPT. It smacked of double standards, many felt, and gave some credence to Ahmadinejad's accusation that America's stance on Iran's nuclear programme was purely political.

long Iran's nuclear partner, tried to arrange a compromise deal – first that Russia would supply the enriched fuel, then possibly that Iran would be allowed to make small amounts of nuclear fuel on Iranian soil. In the face of Iran's determination to press ahead, even these talks broke down.

Deadlock

By the beginning of March, the war of words between the USA and Iran was reaching boiling point. US Vice President Dick Cheney warned that continued defiance from Iran would bring 'meaningful consequences', while US ambassador to the UN John Bolton hinted at 'painful consequences' for Iran if it goes ahead with uranium enrichment. In return, Iran threatened that it could inflict 'harm and pain' on America to match anything the US could do. 'The United States has the power to cause harm and pain', the Iranians said. 'But the United States is also susceptible to harm and pain. So if that is the path the US wishes to choose, let the ball roll.' If the US succeeded in imposing sanctions on Iran, the implication was, Iran would retaliate by barring all oil exports – sending oil prices skyrocketing and creating a world energy crisis.

Exasperated by the lack of progress, the IAEA eventually decided to refer the matter to the UN Security Council. The Iranians, far from being intimidated, began to step up their programme. As the five members of the Security Council wrangled over how to bring it into line, Iran raced ahead with its plans for uranium enrichment. By late March 2006, it had got its first centrifuges working at Natanz. By the end of the year, it plans to have 3,000 centrifuges up and running. British Foreign Office officials warned that Iran could be able to make a nuclear bomb by the beginning of 2007.

The American hostage crisis, Iranian support of terrorist groups like Hezbollah, Ayatollah Khomeini's fatwa against Salman Rushdie, Ahmadinejad's threat to wipe Israel off the map, and many other things have combined to give Iran a disturbing image in the West. Although few European politicians concur entirely with George Bush's view of Iran as part of an axis of evil, they feel only too wary about Iran's potential for causing havoc in the Middle East. But just how true is this image?

Iran is certainly in the grip of a repressive regime. The Islamic Republic has always, in its way, shown itself just as ruthless in suppressing dissent as the Pahlavi shahs, and Ahmadinejad has presided over a renewed crackdown that may become as harsh and restrictive as anything since the 1980s. There's no doubt that the hardline clerics have regained at least some measure of control. Meanwhile, the belligerent approach of Ahmadinejad and his colleagues to the nuclear arms issue, and their proclamations against Israel, give the impression that Iran is in the hands of fanatics.

Yet Iran is not like Afghanistan. It is a sophisticated country with experience of democracy dating back over a century. Iranians may have been deeply disappointed by Khatami's failure to deliver reform, but his election twice showed just what a desire there is for change. The population is young, and though they do not dare protest openly, there is a subversive subculture behind closed doors, helped by the internet and satellite TV. Many young people in Iran, and Iranian exiles outside, are eager for change.

The Islamic Revolution has succeeded in opening education to huge numbers – especially women, who now make up almost two-thirds of the university population. Although most of these young women still wear the chador and behave entirely according to Islamic diktats, their

Shirin Ebadi

In 2003, an Iranian won the Nobel Peace Prize for the first time. She was human rights lawyer Shirin Ebadi. Born in 1947, she graduated with a law degree from Tehran University and became Iran's first female judge. She was forced to resign after the Islamic Revolution, but became an activist for democracy and the legal rights of refugees, women and children. She also became famous for representing writers and dissidents killed by the regime in the 1990s. Her investigation into the murders of Dariush and Paryaneh Foruhar in 1998 led her to point the finger at 'rogue agents' in the Intelligence Ministry, and the minister was forced to resign. Hardline ayatollahs accuse Ebadi of trying to undermine Islam, but she says: 'There is no difference between Islam and human rights.'

education has given them a glimpse, at least, of something more. Many, it seems likely, are not so willing to go along with the patriarchy of the mullahs as they once were.

For the moment, such aspirations must remain largely unspoken with the hardliners in control. Yet Iran's government institutions are far from being one-dimensional. The Majlis, for all that the candidates are vetted, does contain a measure of democracy, and there remain more reform-minded politicians within the power structure. Rafsanjani, although he was beaten by Ahmad-inejad, remains a force to be reckoned with. Even among the religious scholars, there are senior voices urging a more tolerant path, such as the ageing Ayatollah Montazeri. It remains to be seen whether their voices will eventually be heard.

One thing many commentators agree on, though, is that tough measures against Iran might only help to unite the people behind their leaders. This is why many are urging the UN Security Council to be very cautious as it debates what to do about Iran's nuclear programme. Precipitate action could drive Iran in precisely the wrong direction.

Yet it's not only the hawks within the US government that are urging 'consequences' – by which they mean sanctions – if Iran insists on going ahead with its nuclear enrichment programme. Distrust of Iran is so widespread in America that even Democrats are calling for tough measures. Indiana Democrat Senator Evan Bayh urged the Bush government not to dally, saying: 'We have wasted valuable time, diverted resources and ignored this problem at our peril ... No one wants to forestall the need to use military force more than I do, but if we are to do so, we must act now.' (Reported in the *New York Times*, 20 January 2006.)

There's no doubt that the USA has shown an animosity towards Iran beyond that of its Western counterparts. Americans never quite understood just how bitter Iranians felt about the American part in the 1953 coup and their 25 years of support for Muhammad Reza Shah, so they were deeply stung by the hostility towards them shown by the Tehran embassy hostage episode, and the Beirut bombings. There were real consequences, too, as the Islamic Revolution cost America its most secure foothold in the Middle East, a major market for US weapons and a secure source of oil. As Stephen Kinzer says: 'These events left Americans feeling deeply wronged. Many believe the Iranian regime has escaped the punishment it deserves. They are still looking for a way to inflict it.'

The Iranians, for their part, still hold a grudge against America, not only for its support for the shahs, but for the massive support it gave Iraq during the Iran–Iraq war. With hardliners in power in both Tehran and Washington, the prospects of a meaningful compromise might seem remote.

The European members of the UN Security Council, along with Russia and China, while exasperated with Iran's intransigence on the nuclear issue, are treading a more cautious path. British Foreign Secretary Jack Straw has been keen to take a more diplomatic tone, saying: 'Our message is that we want the Iranian people to enjoy the benefits of civil nuclear power, and we support their aspirations for a freer, more democratic and prosperous Iran.' The linking of the nuclear issue to increased democracy had a clear message for Iranians. Meanwhile, German Chancellor Angela Merkel reminded George Bush on a visit to Germany about her experience of sanctions in East Germany. The East German people had no problem with sanctions that hurt the Communist leaders, she said, but 'if we ran out of oranges or bananas, then we didn't like it'.

In an attempt to get around this problem,

American diplomats are talking in terms of 'smart measures'. By this they mean sanctions targeted at Iranian government officials, and not at the people – including such things as freezing bank accounts held in the West and restricting foreign travel. Iran is so bent on its nuclear programme now, though, that such measures will probably have little effect – especially since President Ahmadinejad is a simple man from a poor background who drives a 30-year-old Peugeot or rides a bike, and who, until he became President, maybe went abroad only once, on an assassination trip to Vienna.

Guardian journalist Polly Toynbee argues that accepting the inevitability of Iran's nuclear programme, then talking to them to minimise the damage, is the only viable way forward. She cites the Aesop fable of the Sun and the Wind as instructive: when they competed to get a man's coat off, the full force of the wind only made the man button up his coat against the cold, while the warmth of the sun persuaded him to take it off himself. (*Guardian*, 7 February 2006)

Ironically, it may be that America and Iran will find that they have mutual interests after all, in Iraq. For Iran, the American-led invasion of Iraq was a godsend. It brought them all they wanted there – the toppling of Saddam and the increased role of Shi'ites – without them having to lift a finger. Suddenly Iran became the stable, dominant force in the Middle East, and its influence in Iraq, through the majority Shia population, became huge. Rather than trying to destabilise the country, Iran played a huge part in keeping the Shi'ite-dominated south of Iraq more under control. Indeed, even the Americans began to see that Iran could be a help here, not a hindrance.

For 25 years, American distrust of Iran has been so vehement that the US government has refused to even negotiate openly with it. The Iranians had an equal distaste for talking to the Americans. Then, late in March 2006, the Americans arranged to open negotiations with Iran about Iraq. Remarkably, Ayatollah Khamenei announced that the talks had his blessing. Diplomats around the world wondered if some other topics might come up in discussions.

Like two school playground rivals, they squared off. George Bush said that in the talks, US officials would show Iran 'what's right or wrong in their activities inside of Iraq'. Khamenei said: 'If the talks mean opening the way for bullying and imposition by the deceitful part [the Americans], then they will be forbidden.' But at least they were beginning to talk.

Iran Issues

BASIC FACTS

Population: 70.5 million (2005)
Major language: Farsi (Persian)
Major religion: Shia Islam
Currency: Rial
GNI per capita: US $2,500 (World Bank, 2005)
Life expectancy: 69 (men); 72 (women)

The people of Iran

After the Islamic Revolution in 1979 and the war
with Iraq, the Islamic regime campaigned inten-
sively to increase the country's population. They
succeeded so well that in the decade between
1976 and 1986, Iran's population doubled. If
growth had continued at the same rate, Iran's
population would have hit 108 million by 2006.

The regime realised just how disastrous this
could be, with the country's resources already
stretched to breaking-point. So they embarked on
an astonishingly effective campaign to slow birth
rates. This included stopping maternity benefits
for families with more than three children, and

requiring couples to go to contraceptive classes before they married. Contraceptive pills are widely available at pharmacies, and condoms are handed out free at health clinics. The result is that Iran's population growth slowed dramatically in the 1990s, and its population is now only just over 70 million. This means that well over half Iran's population are now young adults, and about 30 per cent are children under fifteen. The proportion of Iranians who clearly remember life under the Shah is now tiny.

Nearly all the population growth has occurred in towns. Just 30 years ago, Iran was predominantly rural. Now two thirds of Iranians live in cities, and over a fifth live in Tehran alone.

The vast majority of Iranians speak Farsi and call themselves Iranian, but there's a rich range of ethnic backgrounds among them. About half are Persian or Farsi. The Persians are descendants of the Elamite and Aryan tribes who migrated here about 4,000 years ago to settle on the Iranian plateau.

The second largest group in Iran are commonly called 'Turks'. They are the Azaris, who make up about a quarter of Iran's population. They speak Azari Turkish, which is a dialect mixing Farsi with Turkish, but they are Shi'ites, unlike the mostly Sunni Turks. They are well known as *bazaari*, and their distinctive voices can be heard bargaining hard in many Iranian bazaars. Most Azaris live in the border provinces in the north-west of Iran, bordering Azerbaijan. Some still have relatives inside Azerbaijan, but long years of border control have weakened ties.

The third largest group is the Kurds, who make up about 10 per cent of the population. They are descended from the Medes, and so have probably lived in the region longer than any other people. Traditionally, the Kurds are nomadic people living in the mountainous west of the country, especially Kordestan. They have largely resisted the Iranian governments' efforts, both before and after 1979, to integrate with the rest of the nation. Sometimes this has led to bloody confrontations. Discrimination keeps them poor, with some of the worst social conditions in Iran. Each year, their clamour for cultural and political autonomy falls on deaf ears. Some Kurds want to establish an independent Kurdish state along with their fellow Kurds in neighbouring Iraq and Turkey.

Making up about 2 per cent of the population each are the Arabs, who live mainly along the Gulf coast, the Lors, the Turkic Turkmen of the north-east, and the Sunni Baluchis of desert-like Baluchistan, famous for their camel races.

The Pahlavi shahs continually tried to make Iran's nomadic tribes settle. Yet there remain considerable numbers of nomads in Iran. About half the Lors and half the Baluchis are nomadic. So too are the Qashqai and Bakhtiari.

The government of Iran

Iran's intricate, strange system of government combines both Western-based democratic institutions and government by the religious jurists. On the one hand is the President and the Majlis, the parliament elected, in theory, by the people. On the other, there are the Supreme Leader and a variety of clerical groups who wield tremendous power, both to veto initiatives from the Majlis and to select candidates. Ever since the Islamic Revolution, there has been a continual battle between these two sides of the Iranian government. At the moment, it looks like the conservative clerics have the upper hand.

The democratic instutions

All Iranians are eligible to vote, and in the 1997 elections for President Khatami, about 80 per cent of those who could vote did. But as disillusion set in, less than 60 per cent voted in 2005 when Ahmadinejad came to power.

The President is elected for four years, and can serve a maximum of two terms – though he can return after a break, as Rafsanjani tried to do in 2005. In theory, Iran's president has much the same executive function as any Western president. In practice, nearly everything he does is strongly guided by the clerics and the Supreme Leader. It is the Supreme Leader who controls the army and sets the defence and foreign policy agenda. Again, in theory, anyone can stand as President. However, the Guardian Council vets all candidates.

Although it must be approved by the Majlis, the President selects his own cabinet. For the first time in 2005, Ahmadinejad – the first non-clerical president – selected a cabinet with only two clerics. It contained no women.

The Majlis has 290 members, elected by popular vote every four years. In 2000, reformist candidates such as those belonging to the Iran Participation Party had the majority, but the 2004 elections swung the balance back in favour of the hardliners, who nominated Gholamali Haddad-Adel as speaker, Iran's first non-cleric speaker.

The clerical institutions

Besides the Supreme Leader, there are two main elements involved in the clerical side of the Iranian government: the Guardian Council and the Assembly of Experts.

The Guardian Council is where the real power lies. The twelve members of the Council are the most powerful men in Iran besides the Supreme Leader. The Guardian Council has to give its approval to every law passed by the Majlis, and can overturn any that it considers un-Islamic. It also vets all presidential candidates and all candidates for the Majlis – and the experts for the Assembly of Experts. Six of the Council members are clerics appointed by the Supreme Leader, six are appointed by the jurists in Qom. Every three years, half the members stand down, so that each member serves for a total of six years. With hardliners in the majority in the Guardian Council at the moment, reformists find it very difficult to make headway.

The Assembly of Experts is a body of 86 clerics whose task is to choose the Supreme Leader and monitor his performance. The balance of power in the Assembly is very much in the hands of the conservatives at the moment, and it's led by the hardline Ayatollah Al Meshkini. However, the current deputy is the reformist ex-president Rafsanjani.

The Supreme Leader is the role taken by Ayatollah Khomeini in the aftermath of the 1979 revolution, and by Ayatollah Khamenei since Khomeini died in 1989. As the conduit between God and the Shia people of Islam, the Supreme Leader has the final say on pretty much everything. He appoints half the Guardian Council, approves the President and commands the armed forces, but his influence can be even greater. In theory, the President comes second to the Supreme Leader in power, but it depends on the mood of the Supreme Leader. When Rafsanjani was president, Khamenei intervened little. When Khatami became president, Khamenei effectively stifled most of his initiatives.

Shari'ah law

Since Islam demands total submission to the will of God, the will of God, as revealed by the Prophet Mohammad, provides the basis of law in many Islamic countries. This Islamic law is called Shari'ah.

Prior to 1979, Iran's laws had been largely secular, with strictly Islamic rules applying only to things like marriage. But under the 1979 constitution, all judges in Iran were required to base their judgements on Shari'ah. Then, in 1982, the Iran Supreme Court struck out any law that did not conform to Shari'ah. Finally, in 1983, the Majlis incorporated punishments indicated by Shari'ah. This included the concept of *qisas*, under which victims are allowed to retaliate against violent crimes, like for like. It also included six crimes for which the punishment is fixed (*hadd*): death for apostasy and highway robbery; amputation of the hand for theft; death by stoning for adultery; 100 lashes for sex with a married person; 80 lashes for an unproved accusation of unchastity; and 80 lashes for drinking alcohol. Beyond the hadd crimes, punishment is up to the courts.

It's hard to know just how many sentences have been carried out under the hadd rules, because they are not always verifiable in the West. In June 2005, the Iranian daily newspaper *Etemaad* reported that a young man was to have his eyes cut out under the Shari'ah law of qisas for throwing acid during a fight – accidentally, he said – and blinding someone. Western news agencies have also picked up reports in the Iranian press of hundreds of women stoned to death for adultery and prostitution, and even of one woman hurled off a ten-storey building. In an interview with *Le Figaro* on 10 September 1994, President Rafsanjani was asked if such stonings take place. He replied: 'No, no such thing exists in Iran. This has been fabricated to damage us.' Some government officials admit that it does happen, but only in very remote villages.

The Iranian media

Under President Khatami there was considerable freedom of the press in Iran, and both Iranian newspapers of most shades of opinion and Western newspapers were available in Tehran. Since 2004, the conservatives have clamped down. Many reformist publications have been closed down and their writers and editors jailed. All the same, some mildly reformist newspapers like *Aftab-e Yazd* (Sun of Yazd), *Etemaad* (Confidence) and *Shargh* (East) are still running. All in all, there are twenty or so major national dailies, the biggest of which is the state broadcast network IRIB's *Jaam-e Jam* (Jam's Cup).

Iranians watch a lot of TV. Officially, TV is provided by the state network IRIB's four-channel network, and its youth channel is very popular. Unofficially, many Iranians watch foreign satellite channels. Although dishes are illegal, the authorities mostly turn a blind eye. Channels run by exiles in the US are an important source of dissident opinion.

Ahmadinejad has closed many of Iran's internet cafés, but the internet remains a major source of uncensored information for about 7 million Iranians. Service providers are not allowed to give access to sites deemed pornographic or anti-Islamic. Nonetheless, many young people are adept at communicating dissident ideas over the net via blogs.

Oil and gas

Oil has long been Iran's major resource, and one of the prime reasons for the West's interest in the country. Iran's oil reserves are truly gigantic. There are at least 125 billion barrels of this black gold beneath Iran – about a tenth of all the world's known reserves. Only Saudi Arabia has more.

Oil extraction and processing dominate the Iranian economy to a huge degree. Over 80 per cent of the country's entire export earnings (about $45 billion) come from oil, and almost half the Iran government's income comes from the government-owned National Iranian Oil Company. Most of the oil comes from six super-giant fields in the south-west of the country, in lozenges between the Zagros mountains and the

Tigris river. Oil extracted here is piped to Kharg Island on the Persian Gulf, or to the vast refinery at Abadan, destroyed during the Iran–Iraq war but now completely rebuilt. All the same, Iran has a shortage of refinement facilities – partly because of US sanctions – so it has to import about $4.5 billion of petrol every year. Ironically, because the state subsidises petrol, a great deal is smuggled out again. Cheap petrol has also led to high consumption, and helped Tehran become one of the most polluted cities in the world.

Iran has huge natural gas reserves too – about a tenth of the world's entire reserves, second only to Russia. In recent years, the exploitation of these has become much more important. Most of the gas so far has come from the Elborz mountains, and from Khorasan, but there are vast deposits yet to be fully developed beneath the Persian Gulf and the Caspian Sea. Much of the gas is piped through the two giant Iranian Gas Trunk lines that cross the country, to link into supplies to new pipes being built in eastern Europe, Russia, Pakistan, Turkey and India. The US has used its influence to block the building of pipelines across Iran.

Economy

The Iranian economy is dominated by oil and natural gas extraction, which provides over half of Iran's GDP. Manufacturing and mining provide about 20 per cent of GDP, agriculture about 12 per cent, and trade about 12 per cent. The major manufactures include Iran's long-famous hand-made carpets, as well as chemicals, food products and consumer items like cars. The major crops are wheat, sugar beet, sugar cane, potatoes, rice and barley, besides fruit such as apricots and the famous Shiraz grapes.

Further Reading

Searching for Hassan, Terence Ward, Anchor Books, 2002

Shah of Shahs, Ryszard Kapucinski, Vintage, 1992

All the Shah's Men, Stephen Kinzer, Wiley, 2003

The Iranians, Sandra Mackey, Plume Books, 1998

Iran: Essential Guide to a Country on the Brink, Encyclopaedia Britannica, 2006

Modern Iran, Nikkie R. Keddie, Yale, 2003

What Went Wrong?, Bernard Lewis, Oxford University Press, 2002

My Uncle Napoleon, Iraj Pizishkad, translated by Dick Davis, Random House, 2006

We Are Iran, Nasrin Alavi, Portobello Books, 2005

Reading 'Lolita' in Tehran, Azar Nafisi, Fourth Estate, 2004

The Mantle of the Prophet, Roy Mottadeh, Oneworld, 2000

The Secret of Laughter: Fairytales and Folk Tales from Ancient Persia, Shusha Guppy, I.B. Tauris, 2005

Tehran Blues, Kaveh Basmenji, Saqi Books, 2005

Ancient Persia, Josef Wiesehofer, I.B. Tauris, 2001

The Persian Expedition, Xenophon, Penguin Classics, 1967

Persian Fire, Tom Holland, Little, Brown, 2005

Bird Flu: Everything You Need to Know

John Farndon

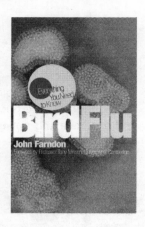

A bird flu pandemic is inevitable – so we are told. First identified in China, this apparently merciless virus which originated in chickens has the potential to mutate, possibly killing thousands, even millions, of people. But how accurate is this picture? Is it a panic created by the media or a genuine threat against which we should protect ourselves immediately – and how can we do this?

Whether you are worried about the implications of bird flu for you and your family, or you are simply interested in learning more than what you see and read in the media, this book is for you.

Paperback £5.99

ISBN: 1 84046 749 5

China: Friend or Foe?

Hugo de Burgh

China is growing phenomenally, with half the world's cranes currently on its soil. Its 1.3 billion people have around 300 million mobile phones and a purchasing power second only to the US, although, especially in rural areas, there is widespread poverty. Government censorship is a fact of life – with 30,000 workers manning a firewall restricting citizens' access to the internet.

Yet few in the West know much about China. Popular press coverage is limited to stereotypes, the serious media to economics and business, and that's about it. What does China mean to the rest of the world?

Hugo de Burgh explores key questions to uncover whether China is a friend to be welcomed or a foe to be guarded against.

Accessible, straightforward and often astonishing, *China: Friend or Foe?* is the first popular exploration of one of the biggest issues of the next hundred years.

Paperback £7.99

ISBN 10: 1 84046 733 9 ISBN 13: 978 1840467 33 8

Everything
You Need
to Know

**Arresting books providing essential
background to topics making the news.**

Everything You Need to Know is a brand-
new occasional series from **Icon Books**.
Produced very quickly in reaction to world
events, each book will delve beneath the
headlines to give you the crucial facts
and real debates behind the stories
of the moment.

For more information, visit:
iconbooks.co.uk/everything